J. Lebron Mcbride, PhD

Living Faithfully
with Disappointment
in the Church

Pre-publication
REVIEW . . .

"**C**lergy and laity alike should be grateful to J. Lebron Mcbride for penning this encouraging book in an age when disappointment with the church seems to be the order of the day. Denominational strife, dissension within congregations, and general apathy have pervaded the church to the extent that too many of them now fail to provide meaning and spiritual vitality in the lives of Christian people. Mcbride's book is a powerful and honest appraisal of the church that offers a number of solutions for overcoming the disappointment and finding renewed hope within the church itself.

Living Faithfully with Disappointment in the Church is helpful precisely because it is realistic about the challenge, recognizing that churches do stumble because of human and institutional frailty. Mcbride points to the problems of control, close-mindedness, isolation, and codependency that often twist and pervert the gospel of Jesus Christ. He speaks to the need for openness, honesty, and flexibility among church members in order to ensure or re-gain congregational health. His clarion call is for an honest assessment of one's own particular church, warts and all, and for personal confession and repentance as an essential step in the recovery of a healthy congregation. Perhaps most important, Mcbride's book should lead to dialogue among church members. He provides a set of questions at the end of each chapter that probe to the very heart of the problem and point toward solutions.

His final chapter is a testimony to the potential of the church to become the very institution that God has intended for it to be from the beginning—a place where human beings discover their true identities and learn how to live faithfully in relationship and in community. Church leaders will find the book to be a great resource that can move congregations toward serious introspection and that can serve as a foundation for reenergizing the faithful."

Robert N. Nash Jr., PhD
Dean, School of Religion
and International Studies,
Shorter College,
Rome, Georgia

Living Faithfully
with Disappointment
in the Church

THE HAWORTH PASTORAL PRESS®
Haworth Series in Chaplaincy
Andrew J. Weaver, Mth, PhD
Editor

Living Faithfully with Disappointment in the Church

J. LeBron McBride, PhD

The Haworth Pastoral Press®
An Imprint of The Haworth Press, Inc.
New York • London • Oxford

For more information on this book or to order, visit
http://www.haworthpress.com/store/product.asp?sku=5355

or call 1-800-HAWORTH (800-429-6784) in the United States and Canada
or (607) 722-5857 outside the United States and Canada

or contact orders@HaworthPress.com

Published by

The Haworth Pastoral Press®, an imprint of The Haworth Press, Inc., 10 Alice Street, Binghamton,
NY 13904-1580.

Portions of this book were first published in *Spiritual Crisis: Surviving Trauma to the Soul* by J. LeBron
McBride, © 1998 by The Haworth Press, Inc. used by permission of The Haworth Press, Inc.

Some sections of this book first appeared in *The Pastoral Forum,* used by permission of The Pastoral
Institute, Columbus, Georgia.

The original version of Chapter 6 appeared as "Preventing Burnout Through Spirituality" in *The
Counselor,* 9(3), pp. 10-13, 1991, used by permission.

Unless otherwise noted, Scripture verses are from *The Holy Bible, New International Version,*
© 1973, 1978 by the International Bible Society, used by permission of Zondervan Bible Publishers.

Cover design by Kerry E. Mack.

Library of Congress Cataloging-in-Publication Data

McBride, J. LeBron.
    Living faithfully with disappointment in the church / J. LeBron McBride.
        p. cm.
    Includes bibliographical references and index.
    ISBN-13: 978-0-7890-2621-7 (hard : alk. paper)
    ISBN-10: 0-7890-2621-X (hard : alk. paper)
    ISBN-13: 978-0-7890-2622-4 (soft : alk. paper)
    ISBN-10: 0-7890-2622-8 (soft : alk. paper)
    1. Church controversies. I. Title.

BV652.9.M33 2005
250—dc22

                                                                          2004024999

To all those sincere persons who have loved the church and have been disappointed, disillusioned, and discouraged by it. You are not alone. My hope is that you may come to try the church again, in part, through the pages of this book.

To First Christian Church (Disciples of Christ) of Rome, Georgia, whose members and friends have renewed their love and energy for the church and have set upon a course of ministry modeled after the compassionate service and acceptance of Christ. You give me greater faith in what the church can become.

ABOUT THE AUTHOR

J. LeBron McBride, PhD, is Senior Minister at First Christian Church (Disciples of Christ) and is Director of Behavioral Medicine and a faculty member at Floyd Medical Center's Family Practice Residency Program in Rome, Georgia. He is also an associate clinical professor at Mercer University School of Medicine in Macon and assistant clinical professor at the Medical College of Georgia. He is a licensed marriage and family therapist, a clinical member and approved supervisor in the American Association of Marriage and Family Therapists, a Fellow in the American Association of Pastoral Counselors, and a Certified Family Life Educator with the National Council of Family Relations. Dr. McBride is the author of numerous journal articles and book chapters, and his first book, *Spiritual Crisis: Surviving Trauma to the Soul,* was published in 1998 by The Haworth Pastoral Press. Dr. McBride, in addition, is author of the forthcoming Haworth books *Family Behavioral Issues in Health and Illness* and *Pastoral Care from the Pulpit: Meditations for Encouragement.*

CONTENTS

Foreword

I wish I'd had this book when I faced disillusionment in my church of origin.

Some years ago, when I was starting out in pastoral ministry, a leader in my congregation asked to see me. Out spilled an anguished tale of his own sense of betrayal and disappointment at the hands of denominational leadership.

"You're a rising young pastor," he said drearily, looking me in the eye. "You have great potential. But you're also idealistic. One day this denomination will hit you, and hit you hard."

That will never happen to me, I thought, waving the remark away, as if I could dismiss it by mere gesture.

But it did. Fifteen years later a theological controversy swept over the denomination. I was teaching at a denominational college at the time. I found myself moving—I like to think, growing—in one theological direction, while the denomination seemed to be moving in another. After several years of unbearable conflict, I finally, painfully, decided to leave the denomination.

It was the most difficult decision of my life. Looking back, as McBride says of his own similar experience, I wouldn't want to repeat those years, but neither would I remove them from my history. The conflict in my denomination, and even more within my own soul, opened me to new spiritual experiences and to a new home in two—not merely one—wonderfully freeing denominations.

The past three decades have reminded us that churches can hurt as well as heal. There is such a thing as "toxic" faith, a faith community that poisons one's spiritual life. There are dysfunctional, negative, harmful religious communities. There are potentially destructive theological systems that inevitably damage the soul of those who cling to them.

This book reminds us that it is helpful to face these painful truths realistically. Even more helpful for one caught in a dysfunctional religious community is to recognize it and to seek resolution. The normalizing of such struggles is itself liberating.

What does one do when spiritually crippling disillusionment sets in?

McBride provides a "guide to the perplexed," to recall Maimonides' famous book by that name. He speaks to lay Christians, to clergy, to anyone who has felt the sharp edges of the church's "shadow side."

He sees tremendous potential in the church. Where else is there to go? he asks. I would agree. One is reminded of a similar question put to Jesus in the gospel of John. "Lord, to whom can we go? You have the words of eternal life" (John 6:68, NRSV). No community on earth has within it more potential for forgiveness, acceptance, and healing. Despite its blundering, it is the real last, best hope of humanity.

Jerry Gladson, PhD
Senior Minister
First Christian Church (Disciples of Christ)
Marietta, Georgia

Preface

The children's hand and finger illustration of "Here's the church, here's the steeple, open the door and see all the people" is not the whole truth. "All" the people are not present in the church. Many no longer set foot in the place where they once experienced joy and peace. For many, it is not that their theology has changed, but that they have been disappointed and disillusioned with the church.

Why has this happened to so many? There are multiple reasons. Some have to do with the institution of the church, whereas others have to do with people problems. Although I am critical of aspects of the church, I write from the perspective of a person who remains an active member. I no longer expect the church to be as perfect as I once did, but I do want it to improve. I am no longer as idealistic about the members of the church, but I do want to see us care more deeply for one another.

Many good institutions today are doing good deeds and providing a sense of community; to some extent the church has lost its dominant role in this area. Churches have done tremendous good for our world. Many of the caring institutions we have today originated with religious movements. Yet the church is beset with its own "shadow side" that handicaps and hampers its great potential. In these pages I seek to openly address this shadow side. Another recurring theme is the danger of controlling and legalistic systems that stifle individuality and identity. I write about the aspects of the church that have caused pain to sincere persons as well as some of the human conditions that create problems in the church. It appears to me that if we can be more open, honest, and realistic then, and only then, we can move toward more compassionate, accepting, caring, and healthy ways of being the church. A church that is functioning well can live faithfully with its humanity.

When I wrote my first book, *Spiritual Crisis: Surviving Trauma to the Soul,* which was academic and written for clergypersons and counselors, several people suggested that I write a similar book for the general public. This is that book. It includes some of the relevant sections from *Spiritual Crisis*; other portions have been simplified and reorganized, and new sections have been added. Much has not been said in this book, because others have already said it better than I ever could. However, I believe this work makes a significant contribution and will speak to the hearts of those who continue to struggle with how best to serve God through the church and how the church can best assist them on their spiritual journey.

My hope is that this book will be used to generate many small group discussions and debates about the challenges faced by the church. I have provided questions for the beginning of such discussions at the end of each chapter. If you have no group for such discussions, the questions can be used for your own private reflections on the church.

Christ remains wonderfully attractive and supremely intriguing to many of us. His authenticity and genuineness startle us. His deeply felt compassion, even for the marginalized of society, humbles us. His communion with his God, as opposed to cold and rigid religion, inspires us. His invitation and acceptance of all people motivates us. His focus on what matters, rather than on the superficial, orients us. The church should mirror this Christ, but it too often fails at the task. To many people the church is simply bricks and mortar devoid of the spirit of Christ. Yet the weak attempts by the church, in its better moments, to manifest Christ is what keeps others in the church. We have no other place to go that offers so much potential even in the midst of human blunderings and failings.

I certainly do not write as an authority or as one who has all the answers. I write as a fellow traveler who has had his own share of broken expectations and intense struggles in the church. I hope you will benefit from my reflections and comments regarding the approach/avoidance relationship many of us have with the church.

May we all learn to enjoy the journey better despite the challenges we confront along the pathway. May the following pages bring comfort and direction to many weary travelers; peace be to you.

Acknowledgments

I owe much to the members of the churches where I have ministered and to the clients I have counseled. They have taught me much of what is in this book. My loving wife, Debbie Walden-McBride, and my friend, Danny Mueller, reviewed the manuscript and gave much needed guidance. My colleague, friend, and associate minister at First Christian Church (Disciples of Christ), Horace Stewart, has been and is a wonderful fellow traveler with whom to reflect, struggle, question, laugh, and cry regarding the issues in this work. I am greatly indebted to The Haworth Press for the careful editing by Copy Editor Debra Adleman and Senior Production Editor Peg Marr. However, the responsibility for the final product, with all its shortcomings, falls fully upon me.

Chapter 1

When Churches Stumble

"I feel so betrayed," he stated with quivering lips as he clenched the threadbare arm of his red easy chair. John was telling his story about his church community. A friend had introduced him to the church after he'd lost his job and had no place to turn to for help. The church and his newfound faith had given him the ability to hang on and a sense of belonging he had not experienced previously. Today, however, he was feeling like an outcast who has lost his only friend.

After investing hours and hours of his time and energy, and even a significant amount of his own money, the church board had just shot down John's plans to continue with a special project and activity center for youth. Some of the members were even hostile, according to John. "They were angry and accused me of ignoring everyone over eighteen years old in the church," he reported. "I thought this was God's mission for me. . . . The youth were responding. . . . Now I don't know what to think. It is really confusing and upsetting." Then John muttered in a low voice filled with sadness, "I think the church is pretty useless."

The topics that I have heard most as a minister and as a family therapist are disappointment and disillusionment with the church. Many have felt hurt, wounded, and emotionally bruised by the church. Smuts van Rooyan titled a brief pamphlet about the church "Is the Church a Hole in the Head?" Then he quoted a statement by a friend who had been greatly disappointed by the church: "I need a church like I need poverty or leprosy. You know the greatest hindrance to Christianity is churchism."

Even leaders loyal to the institution voice their struggles and concerns when they refer to the current state of the church: Robert Wilke (1986) wrote in his book *And Are We Yet Alive?*

> We are wasting away like a leukemia victim when the blood transfusions no longer work. . . . Now we are tired, listless, fueled only by the nostalgia of former days, walking with a droop, eyes on the ground, discouraged, putting one foot ahead of the other like a tired old man who remembers, but can no longer perform. (p. 9)

Robert McAfee Brown in his book *The Significance of the Church* quotes a late medieval manuscript that stated: "The church is something like Noah's ark. If it weren't for the storm outside, you could not stand the smell inside" (p. 17).

IDEALISM AND THE CHURCH

John may have initially thought of the church much as one might think of the beginning of a lovers' relationship, that it would fulfill his every need. John found the church when he was very needy, and it seemed to be perfect for him at the time. In family therapy we call the period of initial attraction in a relationship "romantic idealization."

Romantic idealization includes the great expectations and the "wow" parts of a new relationship, which blind us to many flaws. The same often happens in our relationship with the church, only more so because of the magical expectations and powerful unconscious fantasies we project upon it. Then comes the letdown. We find that the church does not respond as we expect each week or especially during a time of life crisis: A leader in the church may be involved in dishonest business deals. The minister may not be as warm and caring as we expect of a person in such a role. Church members sometimes bicker over the silliest things. Motives in the church may appear to be far from those of Christ, and honest questions that go against the status quo are quickly dismissed or ignored.

It just doesn't always go as we expect in the church. John, introduced at the beginning of this chapter, may have been experiencing a political process going on in the church that excluded all ideas not coming from the "old guard." John is an example of someone who idealizes the church and is having great difficulty with the reality that it doesn't always meet all expectations.

Sometimes the myths in Exhibit 1.1 set us up for a letdown. Disillusionment and disappointment hit hard and can precipitate a spiritual crisis. This disillusionment may concern theological positions taken or issues dealing with "proper" Christian behavior, but most often, at the most basic level, it is relationship disappointment. Even though John had invested much in the youth program that was not supported, his main sense of pain was the personal rejection he felt from the church board.

UNITY VERSUS COMMUNITY

To those of us who have heard many of the sermons regarding the early church, another problem is that we often have a distorted view of the early church that elevates the unity of that period to unrealistic proportions. New Testament scholar Paul Achtemeier

EXHIBIT 1.1. Crisis-Making Myths About the Church

- The church is perfect.
- The church has all the answers.
- The church has no answers.
- The church must continue in the same old way.
- The church must change everything.
- The church can meet our every need.
- The church has no cultural and denominational biases.
- The church doesn't have to answer any of its challenges.
- Theology is the greatest spiritual interest of its members.
- The church can no longer be relevant.

(1987) in his book *The Quest for Unity in the New Testament Church* put it this way:

> Unless we are aware of the problems the early church faced concerning its unity, we will inevitably romanticize that period and either give up in despair at the course taken by subsequent developments in the history of the church, or else assume in a naive way that all it takes to recover that lost, original unity is a little good will and some pleasant negotiations. (p. 2)

The early disciples misunderstood the whole purpose of Christ's plan and place in history as they dreamed of an earthly kingdom. They even bickered among themselves about their status in this new kingdom on the night Christ was betrayed. They tucked their tails and ran when Jesus was arrested. They suffered from jealousy, envy, fits of anger, depression, and all of the maladies we fight in our lives. One was even involved in a shady business deal with those seeking to destroy Christ. The church has never been lily white, and it never will be on this earth.

I have always enjoyed the statement attributed to the great preacher of the 1800s, Charles Spurgeon. It is told that a gentleman said to him one day, "I'd become a member of the church if there were not so many hypocrites in it." To this statement Spurgeon replied, with his usual wit, "Come on in, Brother; one more won't matter!" That is the bottom line, isn't it? Imperfect sinners will never create a perfect institution even if it was established by Christ. It has been so from the very beginning, and so will it ever be. And what if the church was a perfect institution? Would we really feel comfortable belonging to it? Would it be a place where we could bare our souls and admit our sins?

I have had my times of disillusionment with the church, but in my quieter reflective moments the church, frail and frustrating as it is, has been a source of comfort with persons struggling against their own sinfulness as I have myself. So often persons such as John have a false image of the unity that is supposed to exist in the church. Unity does not mean uniformity, nor does it always limit controversy. However, Christian unity should indicate that everything be done with a sense of community involved.

THE CHURCH: THE COMMUNITY

The danger is that the church's faults will sidetrack it from claiming its sense of community and thus be bypassed or given up. The remedy, at least from one perspective, is for the church to be the community that is so needed today. In an ideal church, people would be truly concerned for one another and sensitive to one another's hurts, pains, and joys. They would seek to show their caring by loving, listening, and by supportive actions. Compassion would overrule competition. Humility would overrule contention. Each member would be valued and affirmed. This is the sense of community that should be the goal of the church. This is the part of the church that John experienced in the beginning, but was neglected once he had been a member for a while.

People may experience the spiritual through a sense of community. Keith Miller (1965) wrote years ago in his book *The Taste of New Wine*:

> Our churches are filled with people who outwardly look contented and at peace, but inwardly are crying out for someone to love them . . . just as they are—confused, frustrated, often frightened, guilty, and often unable to communicate even within their own families. (p. 22)

Communities that provide unconditional acceptance and love can be a channel through which people find the spiritual. The gospel tells us that God does not establish a relationship with us based on how well we perform or on how much we have it all together, and neither should our communities of worship. Romans 15:7 makes this clear: "Accept one another, then, just as Christ has accepted you."

WHEN THE CHURCH WALKS WITH TWO FEET ON THE GROUND

In summary, the answer to many of the issues that prevent or heal disillusionment with the church are found when the church and its members realize their weaknesses and truly focus on being a community of Christian fellowship. Jurgen Moltmann (1978) in *The Open Church: An Invitation to a Messianic Lifestyle* wrote of the radical sense of acceptance and community that is to exist in the church:

> We are no longer individualists but a congregation in which the one accepts the other in the way that one has already been accepted by Christ. . . . Congregation is rather a new kind of living together for human beings that affirms:
>
> - that no one is alone with his or her problems . . .
> - that no one has to conceal his or her disabilities . . .
> - that one bears the other even when it is unpleasant and there is no agreement. (p. 33)

May we experience the faults and failures of the church as challenges and realities not to be denied. May we, on the other hand, accept the church as being an institution with great potential for acceptance and community. Thus disillusionment can be recognized and accepted in the context of a caring and restoring community of healing. If John, the hurt and frustrated church member mentioned previously, had experienced the church in this way, he might still be worshiping in one of our churches today.

QUESTIONS FOR DISCUSSION/REFLECTION

1. What are some of the precipitators of crisis in the church?
2. Do you think many people are unfairly idealistic about the church?
3. What human dynamics have you seen played out in the church?
4. How can the church best survive in our current society? What adjustments need to be made?
5. Why does change appear to be so difficult for the church?
6. Where have you experienced a sense of Christian community?
7. Describe how you think the church will look in the next decade.
8. What ingredients keep people interested in belonging to a church?
9. How are church members like everyone else in society? Should they be different? If so, how?
10. How do you deal with conflict in the church or with situations in the church that hurt your feelings?

Chapter 2

When Families Feud

We often don't like to accept that God has chosen to work through the human predicament with all its flaws, sins, selfish aims, and competitions. Rabbi Edwin Friedman (1985) has written about churches and synagogues functioning according to the dynamics of family systems. He describes in his book *Generation to Generation* what he calls "live wires loosely flapping about" in the church that come from both the unresolved issues of families of church members and the dynamics of the church family. Thus some religious institutions function as healthier families than others. Certainly, in some churches members exhibit dysfunctional family traits.

BOUNDARIES

Families can have closed, open, or diffuse boundaries. Open family boundaries allow for people to interact freely with others outside the family or to be with only family members. Diffuse (almost nonexistent) family boundaries can cause the family to be so chaotic that no one can tell for sure who is in the family and who is not. Diffuse boundaries also may not provide enough protection and structure, especially for children. On the other hand, closed boundaries put up rigid walls that exclude those outside the family. Closed boundaries can isolate the family; new and important information may not be permitted into the family awareness. In a healthy family, the boundaries can move from diffuse to open to closed according to the needs of the family. For example, in our society normally the couple system is fairly closed while a newly formed couple establishes its identity. Over its life cycle the healthy family usually has open boundaries.

STAGNANT MINDS LEAD TO ISOLATED AND CLOSED CHURCHES

Some churches have very rigid and closed boundaries and do not permit easy access. Visitors may feel this during a brief encounter, or it may take awhile for a newcomer experience the barriers to new ideas or people. Just as closed or isolated family systems tend to become more dysfunctional, so do closed or isolated churches. Such churches become stagnant, and a type of theological incest, caused by inbreeding of ideas and beliefs develops. In such churches members often forget how to think creatively and for themselves. They place their minds in neutral each time they enter the doors of the church. Soon any new idea becomes stuck in the concrete of their murky religious structure.

Healthy churches tend to be open and flexible to new ideas and new members. They can look closely at themselves and laugh at themselves. People who believe differently do not threaten them. They can test the different or new, accept what is good, and reject what is bad. This was John Wesley's attitude, and he refused to let differences of opinion divide: "If thine heart is as my heart, if thou lovest God and all mankind: Give me thine hand" (Outler, 1985, p. 90).

CONTROLLING FAMILIES

Sometimes one family becomes dominant in the church structure and dictates all that is done within the church. Such churches often have closed boundaries, and the controlling family is very selective about who is truly accepted into the church. The old rule that "blood is thicker than water" applies here, or, we might say, "blood is thicker than religious dynamics" in these situations. Most corporations have rules against related persons working in the same departments or some type of limitations on family members working together. This prevents many conflicts and problems in the workplace. However, in the church we can institute no such rule—nor should we—but this leaves the church wide open to the problems of families and family control and conflict. The ruling family's relationships override the spiritual needs of the church, and the dysfunction of the family gets played out.

The Storm family and the Tornado family were among the founding families of The New Testament Peaceloving Church. Initially, the Storm and Tornado families were very close, and there had even been a marriage between a daughter from the Storm family and a son from the Tornado family a few generations back. Unfortunately, the marriage was filled with conflict and finally ended in divorce. During the days leading up to the divorce church members in both families took sides with the spouse who was from their family. Words got ugly and accusations flew back and forth between members of the two families. The marital partners have now long been deceased and the initial arguments and reasons for the divorce are hazy, but the bitterness between the two families continues. Even the election of church officers is filled with competition each year because of the feud. Little is done in the church now because the two opposing sides cannot reach a consensus on any new venture.

A few new members who have recently moved into the area are totally baffled by the inability of the congregation to work together. The new members do not know the history of the fights between the families. Occasionally they witness intense feelings of one church member against another, but they do not understand why such feelings exist. Most new members eventually no longer attempt to be involved and gradually pull away from the church or transfer to another where the weather forecast is not so filled with storms and tornadoes.

Another example of family dynamics getting in the way of the church is when family members are placed in leadership positions because of their relatives instead of their spiritual gifts. Some may be leaders in their family system, but that does not necessarily qualify them to be leaders in the church.

CHURCH BULLIES

Often the church is an arena for the replication of issues that originated in the family. This can happen when members are from a family with a controlling and domineering parent. There may have been conflict between that parent and the children. If such family issues are not worked out during childhood, the children can become adult church members who continue to rebel against anyone in authority.

These people can give ministers and church leaders indigestion. They can be antagonistic about anything and everything. They can ruthlessly tear people apart emotionally and bully others until their own will is accepted by church boards. Sometimes this is done openly and sometimes behind the scenes, destroying the influence of the ministers or leaders.

In larger churches such antagonistic or rebellious people often are not allowed to assert their destructive authority. However, in many small churches they find their niche and work out their dysfunctional purposes. Often they rule and dominate church board meetings and handicap the church's progress. The other members, seeking to be true to their beliefs about meekness and gentleness, do not take a hard stand to oppose such people. Unless churches take a stand against such destructive people, the future of the church can be in serious jeopardy.

It is better to lose such members if they will not respond to appropriate confrontation than to allow them to take the church down with them. Some of these people are deeply insecure and will respond when confronted in a caring but firm manner. When I was working as a local pastor, I always sought to find out who such persons were early in my pastorate and I would make a special effort to establish a relationship with them so that I could later confront them in a caring manner if it became necessary. This also assisted me in attempting to find their good points that could be utilized by the church and kept me from focusing only on their negative, antagonistic qualities.

CHURCH CODEPENDENTS

The family dynamic of dependency is often played out in the church. Many individuals have never felt accepted in their families for who they are, but only for what they do. Others for various reasons become what in today's lingo is called *codependent.* The word *codependent* was coined and spread like wildfire throughout the counseling community a number of years ago. It has been used to describe everything from enabling an alcoholic to being a people pleaser. Even with its hodgepodge of meanings it does touch on some important aspects of people's lives. It usually refers to defining one's worth primarily by what one does or by how one relates to others. There usually is a blurring of boundaries with the person one attaches to out of a desperate need for approval and acceptance. This results in sacrifice of one's identity and needs to the other and usually places extreme demands on the self.

Some individuals become codependent on the church. They look to the church for all their identity, and this can take the place of self-identity or even their true worship of God. They can become centered on the church to the neglect, or in the place of, being centered on God. It is possible for people to become so obsessed with the church for the wrong reasons that they feel dependent on it for survival. These can be wonderful people with beautiful gifts, but they end up going to extremes to the detriment of their own health and spirituality.

Some churches appear to encourage this dependency in an unhealthy way. Much damage has been done to individuals and their families in these situations, all in the name of dedication to the church. Although there is little danger of this happening today because many people go to the other extreme and are distant from church activities, we should be aware of this dynamic. There is a difference between healthy and unhealthy involvement in the church. Churches and cults that swallow up people's individualities as well as their lives can destroy the gifts of the various members and produce robot-like copies of each other. Unity may occur at the expense of true self-identities and gifts.

I write about codependency because the topic is tremendously relevant to many who are disappointed and disillusioned with the church. It is often those who are codependent whom the church uses and abuses. This is not intentional; it happens because so much needs to be done in the church, and the codependents are so ready to do it. At first, and maybe even for years, the codependents feel valued for playing such a needed role. Over time, however, burnout and frustration occur. Codependents are not assertive at saying "no," so more and more tasks are given them. They begin to see that others are not pulling their load. Too often it is difficult for them to delegate, so they continue working alone, which becomes destructive and often leads to bitterness.

Church leaders need to be more sensitive to those good people who tend toward codependency and assist them in setting limits and feeling accepted by the gospel. Some who had a role reversal in childhood in which they were the main nurturers rather than the parents easily fall into the role of knowing the needs of others, but lack an understanding of their own needs. The church can produce weak, anorexic skeletons of soulless Christians clinging to others for identity. This is not God's plan. The historical teaching of Christianity is that God creates us in his image and gives us unique gifts and ways of ministry. The worth of each person as a child of God is secure, and we are not required to perform to be accepted. The gospel communicates a profound sense of worth and dignity for each person that is not achievement or performance based, but is the result of the gift of grace. We are accepted despite our failures and faults. We do not need to be codependent to even the church for our worth and acceptance.

Church members repeat their family dysfunction within the church in numerous ways; although only a few are briefly addressed here, we need to be aware of how family dynamics get played out in the church. Often members do not intentionally seek to be disruptive or destructive. They are just playing the role they are used to playing, reacting to hurts and pains of the past, and seeking ways to feel accepted and loved. We scratch our heads and say, "They are doing the opposite of what would truly help them." Often this is true, and one of the great services the church can furnish, when it is functioning well, is to provide relief from old destructive patterns and give members a new way of living and being in the gospel!

QUESTIONS FOR DISCUSSION/REFLECTION

1. How is the church like a family?
2. How is the church not like a family?
3. What family dynamics have you witnessed in churches?
4. What kind of boundaries should the church have?
5. What are some of the characteristics of antagonistic persons?
6. How do you think the church should deal with someone who is continually antagonistic?
7. Is codependency ever a good thing?

8. How could we be more helpful to people who are co-dependent on the church?
9. How have issues from the family in which you were raised affected your life in the church?
10. How can we be more aware of how family issues intensify conflicts in the church?

Chapter 3

When Beliefs Crumble

Sara experienced the horrific sound of squealing car brakes and crumpling metal as she attempted to avoid the oncoming car. After the cars came to a crashing halt she immediately looked into the backseat to check on her five-year-old son, but the sight was not what she had anticipated. Her son was dead. His car door had taken the brunt of the impact, and, even though he was wearing his seat belt, he suffered a lethal head injury.

After the accident the months slowly turned into years, and Sara struggled to find comfort with her beliefs. She was committed to the Christian faith, but found that some of the ways she approached God and the church had changed. She had lingering doubts and questions: How could God allow her son to be killed? Why did her prayers for her son's protection do no good? Some of the beliefs of the past had crumbled and no longer had meaning. She was afraid to discuss her feelings with her pastor or with any other member of the church for fear they would think she was disloyal to the faith. She silently sat in church and wondered how many others around her kept silent about their innermost feelings and beliefs. Sara did not question that she believed in the teachings of Christ, but she sometimes felt her faith was weak because she no longer believed the way she did before the accident.

A CRISIS CAN BRING FORCED INTROSPECTION

When our world is shaken by events we don't understand, we begin to question our assumptions about life. Often there is an obsessive quality to our questioning and introspection, and we become more reflective and introspective than normal. Like a dog with a bone, when this forced introspection grabs hold it doesn't want to let go until we achieve some resolution or stabilization from our belief system.

A crisis or trauma can bring issues to the mind for which our beliefs have no solutions. For example, Sara may have assumed, in her belief system, that harm would never come to her family because God protected them. The reality of her son's death challenged this assumption to the utmost. Along with the challenge came a realization that her old belief structure did not make allowances for the type of tragedy she had experienced. She had to find a way to adjust her beliefs to deal with this reality.

ADJUSTMENTS TO BELIEF STRUCTURES CAN BE DIFFICULT

Many beliefs change when a belief structure no longer provides adequate answers or satisfies deeper longings for spirituality or fellowship. The initial result can be very disturbing when people realize that their beliefs no longer work. Some find themselves seeking just to stay afloat spiritually. Some give up the quest for spiritual or religious fulfillment. Individual and family psychotherapists have noted that more physical or psychological symptoms occur at critical transitions of the individual or family life cycle. These symptoms can also increase during some belief transitions. People are more prone to withdrawal and introspection, anxiety, depression, anger, obsessive thoughts, and confusion when their belief system is shifting, shaking, or shattering.

Ambivalence or a back-and-forth struggle can also be an aspect of belief changes. Sometimes even a sense of feeling less spiritual occurs if one is moving from a very structured belief system to one that is less structured. Issues are not as clear-cut and defined. One person wrote the following to me during the early days of a transition in her belief system:

I must admit that there are times when I'm not sure what is going on in my head. All I know is that when I think of going back to the "religious experience" of the past, I can't stand the thought. I've found a freedom and a joy that I've never known before, and the more I learn, the better I feel about it. Yet you can't be raised under the "old school" and not fear, from time to time, that you're a heretic.

Beliefs, even of dedicated Christians, do sometimes change or even crumble. It doesn't take a loss as tragic as Sara's to challenge our beliefs. Certainly trauma challenges or shatters beliefs and assumptions about life and God, but our beliefs can also be shaken by less dramatic life events. This doesn't mean that people questioning their beliefs are no longer Christians or that they are being unfaithful. True faith usually questions, often doubts, and sometimes leads in new directions.

THE CHURCH SHOULD BE A SAFE PLACE
FOR HONEST DISCUSSION

In the church we have been too insecure to allow many to truly voice their inner thoughts, and too often we have stifled the very discussions that would prevent disappointment with the church. Our churches do not always provide a safe place for members to discuss their innermost selves and belief struggles. Often little opportunity occurs within religious institutions to verbalize personal struggles with faith. Some churches require blind loyalty or at least the appearance of unquestioning loyalty. As a result, individuals are left to go through honest doubting and searching alone.

Many may give up on the church because they feel that they believe too different from those in the church. While there are also many people who never really assess their faith or wonder about their beliefs, other very dedicated and sincere people experience honest questioning of aspects of their faith. If this has happened to you, don't give up on the church as a whole. Attempt to find a pastoral counselor who will assist you in openly and honestly exploring your beliefs in the confidentiality of the counseling room. The pastor or counselor who allows the verbalizations of such struggles may help smooth transitions so that they do not become destructive or extreme.

BELIEFS CHANGE IN MULTIPLE WAYS

Beliefs can change in several ways. Sometimes beliefs change because of a crisis. Other belief transitions are subtle and occur as a gradual process over many years. Yet other belief transitions are dramatic and are described well by the word *conversion.* A person may be radically transformed, and all may readily see the evidence. Some transitions greatly alter the direction of a person's life, while only a particular view is changed in another's. Sometimes changes in belief are simply incorporated into the way a person has always believed, and there is little evidence of change.

Belief transitions can also precipitate a crisis in the family, church, community, and nation. Families have disowned family members whose beliefs begin to differ from the way the family was indoctrinated. Some churches have been known to expel members who with a spirit of humility asked honest questions. Christ went against the established beliefs and traditions and was called Beelzebub, the prince of demons, and was eventually crucified. Reformers have been stoned and burned at the stake in past ages. The church takes less open forms of censure today, such as subtle isolation and withdrawal from those who challenge it.

BELIEF TRANSITIONS ARE NORMAL,
NOT ABNORMAL

When my son was four and a half years old he made this announcement at the breakfast table: "God lied to me!" Puzzled, my wife and I asked what he meant, and he replied, "I prayed for my booboo to get better last night and it's still on my finger this morning. God lied to me!" At his stage of development, his understanding of prayer was that answers should be instantaneous and miraculous. Most adults would not make the exact assumptions about prayer that a four-year-old makes. Some of our belief changes come with maturation and development. Often in our youth we are much more absolute about all details of our faith and expect to have all the right answers provided. As we mature we realize that we sometimes cannot have such a certainty about some aspects of our faith. For example, as adults we realize that God will not make all our "booboos" or difficulties better overnight. While it is important to be childlike in our faith, it is also important not to be childish.

To take this thinking one step farther, we could say that people mature in various ways and at various rates in their Christian walk. The apostle Paul certainly allows for levels of growth among Christians. People differ in their opinions according to their personal experiences or stage of maturity. What they believe at one stage of the Christian life can change as they mature in their faith or as cultural practices change. This is not necessarily a sign of the end or of apostasy, as some would have us believe, but simply the variability among nonessentials of the faith. Belief transitions are a normal part of individual and spiritual development, and we should expect some adaptation or change along the Christian journey.

Some feel that they must throw the baby out with the bathwater, so to speak, when they confront a situation that doesn't fit nicely into their belief system. They feel if they change in one area then nothing is to be valued from the past. On the other hand, some who are attempting to hold on too tightly to the past will accuse others of abandoning the faith if even a minute change occurs from the way things have always been done. This is another reason we need open and understanding discussions in our churches that do not place blame and shame upon sharing of differing opinions. The community of faith that is honest, truthful, and sincere can provide a balance from extremes on either side.

At the least the church can make the journey more tolerable. Working as a psychotherapist, I have often found that when a person keeps some event or way of thinking entirely internal, it gains and grows in power. Usually, when a person has the opportunity to safely discuss the issue with another person it changes the perspective and lessens the internal struggle. The person's way of thinking may or may not change and certainly the event will stay the same, but somehow sharing and hearing the issue put into audible words makes it more manageable.

MOVEMENT FROM THE STATUS QUO
MAY ENERGIZE

Positive emotions, such as the feeling of freedom described in the New Testament among those who found the gospel and were freed from the condemnation of the law, may be present with belief changes. At times of great religious revival and movement such as the Protestant Reformation, new incentives for spiritual depth are born. Although I am not advocating change for change's sake, new energy may be gained by the excitement of the new or growing beliefs. New associations and friendships are often formed with people of similar beliefs. Energy for incorporating the new ways of believing may move people to new levels of study, meditation, and reflection. A new dedication and a new commitment are often felt by those who incorporate fresh material into their belief systems.

In summary, even religious institutions have not been sensitive enough to the struggle and crisis some experience with belief transitions. While belief transitions can come in various ways and can be a normal phase of spiritual development, they can leave persons with initial feelings of confusion, doubt, and questioning. Churches need to be more sympathetic to the ministry of supporting members through belief transitions. As a result, communities of faith may assist persons in avoiding getting stuck with the status quo or, on the other hand, rejecting everything they once believed. Thereby, members may be energized for greater spiritual experiences.

QUESTIONS FOR DISCUSSION/REFLECTION

1. Does your church really allow open discussion?
2. What have been the taboo subjects you have witnessed in church discussions?
3. Have you ever verbalized your struggles with your faith to another believer?
4. Do you believe that Christians go through belief transitions when they join the church?
5. Can you give any examples of belief transitions that caused a crisis?
6. Does acceptance of Christianity usually precipitate a stressful belief transition as it did for the apostle Paul?
7. What can we do with the things that do not appear to fit logically with our belief systems, but are a part of our reality?
8. Many say we are not to question God; do you believe this statement?
9. What belief confrontations do crises often bring?
10. Give biblical examples of people experiencing a belief transition or belief crisis.

Chapter 4

When Religion Rigidifies

Religion has great potential for goodness, but corrupted religion can bring unrest to the soul. When one looks across the religious landscape, it is shocking to see the vast number of traumas and casualties lying among the holy places. Many traumatic injuries to the psyche occur on religious journeys. People who once centered their lives in their faith have forsaken it, or they have become as lifeless as mannequins in a store window. Some continue to go through the motions that no longer have meaning to them, and others try to flee from the consuming grip of destructive religion.

This chapter focuses on the form versus the essence or, we could say, sick religion versus healthy religion. A crisis occurs when we confuse the form and the essence that can disrupt and arrest our spiritual growth. It can happen slowly over time with little awareness, or it can occur rapidly under powerful influences and control. Regardless, it can hemorrhage our spiritual lives.

In the past few decades we have come to appreciate the impact of traumatic experiences on those who experience them. We have even defined the psychological disorder that results from horrific trauma: post-traumatic stress disorder. While I certainly do not wish to minimize in any way the terrible experiences that many have with various forms of abuse, violence, and war (which may have a component of extreme religion), I have found some less intense parallels in those who experience the trauma of destructive religion. I have also discovered that a purely theological approach to the healing of such persons, while vital, is not as helpful as a holistic approach that includes the psychological and relational aspects as well.

Religion, of course, has had great positive impact. History as well as anthropology and archeology have shown us how pervasive religion is and has been throughout the world. Religion has facilitated the spiritual development of many peoples. Yet religion has a downside when it is used improperly. We are all aware of the great crimes that have been committed in the name of religion. Destructive religion can teach us more about evil than anything else. Bad religion can be just as much of a curse as good religion can be a blessing. However, there is another shadow side that is far more subtle and it can lead to a malady we might call "religious burnout." Religious burnout can occur in any religion, but especially in one that rigidifies as described in this chapter and outlined in Exhibit 4.1.

The phenomenon is most extreme among the cults, although it can occur in all religious movements. However, in the cults one usually finds greater pressure toward conformity and giving up individuality. Initially, new converts may artificially improve their functioning in some areas because they borrow ego strength from the belief system or group. They may become leaders for the "truth." Previously uncommitted persons may become "true believers" ready

EXHIBIT 4.1. Warning Signs of Rigidifying Religion

- When the system becomes more important than the members
- When self-identity and individuality are smothered, stifled, or devoured
- When shame is used to control
- When emotional numbing occurs
- When leaders use coercion instead of invitation
- When questioning is not permitted or is ignored
- When spiritual growth is blocked or stopped
- When authority is used to manipulate
- When most energy is spent maintaining the status quo
- When members are isolated from society
- When the system, leaders, scriptures or other writings, or rituals become more important than a relationship with God
- When leaders are not held accountable
- When the importance of healthy relationships is minimized

to sacrifice anything for the group. Often in this process there is a loss of selfhood, of personality, and of personal freedom.

When such affected people are asked about how they are doing, they will give a positive answer. How could they be an example for "the truth" if they admit to feeling bad? A powerful denial structure is built that screens out whole segments of thoughts and feelings. They begin running on an obsession, a religious high, or what we might call a religious addiction.

ADDICTIVE PROCESSES IN ORGANIZATIONS

We are aware of the danger of abusing drugs and the concept of addiction, as well as how destructive addiction can be. Anne Wilson Schaef in her books *When Society Becomes an Addict* (1988) and (with Diane Fassel) *The Addictive Organization* (1988) gives us insight into how processes rather than drugs become part of addictive systems on which we get hooked. All religious systems have aspects that could be used incorrectly and become addictive processes. Many religious systems even encourage addictive behaviors and are easily used addictively by certain personalities. These can be extremely destructive in some of the same ways that chemical addictions are. These processes can lead to the numbing and shutting down of important aspects of the self and the spiritual life.

Some of the processes of addictive systems that are described by Schaef are as follows: First, there is the process of the promise. By this she means the focus on expectations and the future. This focus gives temporary relief from the present at the expense of keeping people out of touch with the present, and can cause sincere people to neglect their personal needs and personal identity. The present becomes the servant of the future so that present needs and realities can be ignored. Because an element of truth exists in the important principle of delayed gratification, the process of the promise can be used to an extreme and become very destructive. When people do everything for a future reward, such as heaven, the present can take on all sorts of interesting perspectives. Current health issues, relationships, and family connections, for example, can be minimized or neglected. People may begin to function out of magical thinking and expect to be rescued from the present, to the extent that current motivation plummets.

Second, the organization removes all that is different from it. Individuals within such organizations have difficulty saying no. This was discussed in Chapter 2 with regard to codependents in the church. As used here, however, it signifies a greater problem. In an addictive religious organization not only are people encouraged to be codependent, but they are also encouraged to have no identity apart from the group or organization. At times this takes a more covert form in religious organizations such as encouraging members to have no life outside the organization. This can occur slowly and over time to the extent that the church absorbs not only the religious life but the entire family and social life as well. Of course, a balance must be sought here. Religious organizations can provide much-needed activities for members, but I get concerned when any organization positions itself to be the only resource members have.

Closely related to these ideas is external referencing, the third process Schaef discusses. External referencing is the tendency to define the self by focusing outside oneself to the group to which one belongs. Boundaries between the individual and the group become unclear. Individual feelings and desires are surrendered to those of the organization. Members have difficulty setting limits for themselves and differentiating between themselves and the religious system. When answers are only a parroting of the answers of the religious institution, our God-given intellects and spiritual gifts are no longer utilized and valued. Members gradually lose the ability to know what they want, feel, and think. The individual self is devoured.

Encouraging discussion and valuing input from all members appears to me to be vital for a healthy religious organization. This openness encourages personal growth and understanding. With external referencing to authorities, even within the religious system, it is too easy for a few to rigidly control the many. Although most institutions need formal policy structures of some kind, neither the leaders nor the institution should ever be given ultimate or supreme authority.

A fourth process used by the addictive organization in dealing with what it cannot control or understand is invalidation. This occurs when opinions that collide with the organization are ignored or dismissed. This is a means of control and of keeping individuals out of touch with their feelings and experiences. Power-hungry people and institutions often use the technique of invalidation to keep members quiet and in place. I have seen this operating to the extent that very clear presentations are dismissed as if they were never heard; it was as if those dismissing the presentation had plugs in their ears!

Dualism is a fifth process used by addictive organizations and is often found among religious groups. Dualism simplifies situations down to two choices. Often this is an "us and them" or a "good and bad" mentality. This gives a sense of false security at the expense of not allowing more options. It also keeps people from exploring other alternatives. If the organization can accuse any dissenters to the party line of being in the opposing camp, then they can easily be split off as being the enemy. Thus members will be afraid to listen to any challenging opinions no matter how logical or relevant. It is easy for this to advance far beyond meaningful debates to personality attacks and character assassinations.

At times, of course, people need to leave a destructive religious organization. Anyone contemplating doing so after having deeply committed to it and its tenets must consider the timing and impact of such a decision, even if leaving is clearly indicated.

THE AWAKENING

People reach the point of leaving a religious system by various pathways. Certainly leaving is not a psychological trauma for all, but it is for many. Often a gradual awakening or realization occurs, that, without further awkward maneuvering and sidestepping, for them the pieces of the theological structure simply no longer fit together. For those who were once zealots for the cause, this awakening can be a disorganizing confusion and an uncomfortable psychological state because life is no longer a neat package. Such a psychological state has been called *cognitive dissonance* because of its internal conflicts. Most will experience a back-and-forth struggle with or ambivalence about what they have been taught and what they are beginning to understand.

This ambivalence and confusion can become extremely intense as people realize that many of the assumptions and beliefs they have been taught and have believed for years are not correct. Their feelings of helplessness, disorientation, and being overwhelmed are similar to those of people going through trauma. Depression, anxiety, rigidity, and impulsive behaviors may become evident. Anger, despair, shame, guilt, distrust, rage, fear, and irritation may be experienced. Nothing seems normal or secure anymore. Spiritual questioning may become an obsession. The upheaval can be horrific.

A PSYCHOLOGICAL AND SPIRITUAL DANGER ZONE

As one client told me, "My faith has been shaken to the core." The crumbling and failing of assumptions and beliefs that one has lived with create a psychological danger zone. The danger zone can include the following temptations:

- To go back to the old belief structure, not because it is valid again, but to regain a sense of safety (which actually is a false security that will not last)
- To believe that everything spiritual or religious must be thrown away—"throwing the baby out with the bathwater"
- To go to extremes with self-medication or other addictive behaviors to numb out the pain
- To deny any new concepts and to shut out any thinking that brings inner conflict
- To accommodate and rework any new belief system to fit the old system to the extent that it compromises integrity
- To treat those who do not grasp the newfound theological perspectives in a non-Christlike manner
- To get so hung up on theological hairsplitting that a relationship with Christ and the central teachings are neglected (as will be discussed in the next chapter)

Many who go on to become more balanced may first but temporarily move toward some of these dangers. The dangers are very real, however, and they can lead to destruction, especially if continued for too long. They can result in great compromise of the psyche and soul as people shut down important parts of themselves and begin to exist as mechanical robots so that the pain can be suppressed. It is important, of course, not to sit in judgment as to the basic manner or how fast people should progress in their struggle with change. The rate of change is a highly individual matter, depending on such dynamics as the amount of indoctrination one had into the religious structure and how long one has been in the system one is attempting to leave.

EXTREMES ARE NOT ONLY FOUND
IN EXTREME ORGANIZATIONS

Most of the religious organizations and churches that we belong to do not create the extent of trauma described in this chapter, yet some of us know people who are in such religious groups. Unfortunately, the processes described earlier are not only found among the extremes of cults and addictive systems, they are also found lurking about in the religious institutions we attend. Efforts of control, denial, conformity, invalidation, absorption, and so on can impinge upon the self, draining vitality and creativity. As one shuts down parts of selfhood, there can be a tendency to become locked within a narrow range of mechanical behaviors and feelings. The gradual loss of control to the larger system leaves one searching for places to find some feeling of control in life. More often than not, this is found by becoming more controlling and demanding to those nearest, such as family members. No longer is the person acting out of love, but is now acting out of the aggression of knowing the "truth." Often the lives of such affected people and their family members become so stifled that no one experiences life-enhancing spirituality.

A subtle emotional trauma occurs with this loss of selfhood. It may take years for people to realize and admit the negative effects because of the strength of their denial system. Often, however, these people slowly begin to burn out on religion. Resources are taken from them without replenishment, and survival becomes based on emotional numbness. This leaves them empty and spiritually bankrupt. These people become the bruised and wounded who eventually may see life and religion as tasks of futility.

THE PROBLEM OF MISTAKING RELIGION
FOR SPIRITUALITY

The basis of the problem is this: Religion is used in place of spiritual experience rather than as a tool to enhance spiritual development. Form is substituted for essence, conformity overrules individuality, the system crowds out God, rigidity replaces openness, and religion is mistaken for spirituality. Tony Campolo (1988) wrote that when he became a Christian it was not "the world" that almost wrecked his faith, but the stifling expectations and demands of the religious in the church.

A religion in which spirituality is hampered becomes controlling. It doesn't allow individual freedom and independent thinking. Everyone must conform to the status quo and support the accepted party line. Individual creativity is squashed. Members become spiritually numb. Because of the humanity of the church it has this tendency toward losing its focus and spirit. Taking the essence out of religion is like turning a body into a machine. Some of the same things can be done, but the vitality and creative energy are missing.

On the other hand, true spirituality motivates us toward growth and wholeness. It recognizes the freedom of each individual to make up his or her own mind. It affirms the right of all to think for themselves and to live with their own personalities and individualities. Spirituality allows for spontaneous and creative acts of worship. Rather than blunting the emotions and intellect, spirituality encourages the expression of our total humanity.

THE CHALLENGE

The challenge is for us to be willing to break through our own denial system and to assess the contribution our religious organizations may make to the eventual religious burnout of their members. It may be frightening at times to step outside our traditional and prescribed ways of thinking, yet it may be necessary to avoid religious burnout. In contrast to the stifling and smothering of rigidified religion, the freedom of religion that is a conduit for spirituality can be exhilarating and energizing.

QUESTIONS FOR DISCUSSION/REFLECTION

1. What are some roads that may lead to religious burnout?
2. Do you believe it is possible to develop a religious addiction?
3. What ways are our communities of worship similar or dissimilar to cults?
4. How would you differentiate between religion and spirituality?
5. In what ways is your religious system too rigid? In what ways is it too unstructured?
6. How can religion hamper spirituality?
7. How can religion be a component of spirituality or an asset for spirituality?
8. How do we carefully evaluate our own religious institutions while we are a part of them?
9. Do religious institutions have any evident power in our current society?
10. Should religious organizations seek to be in the world but not of it?

Chapter 5

When Leaving Hurts

Disappointment with the church can result from becoming out of harmony with a denomination. It may be that you and your denomination have gradually traveled in different directions, you have changed in theology, or you have come to realize the limitations of the denomination that once met your needs. This chapter is an overview of my personal crisis of denominational identity; some of it is a personal story of the dynamics discussed in Chapter 4. It was a spiritual crisis of horrific magnitude, but it became an opportunity for growth in understanding others, church, religious dynamics, and myself. It is now one of those events that I would never want to repeat, but one that I would not want to remove from my history.

Hopefully, most people can find a way to remain within the religious structure in which they find themselves, but for those in destructive systems or who find no room for growth and ministry in their current organization, the painful process of separation may occur. This chapter is pertinent especially for those considering such a transition; I encourage a careful and prayerful assessment of options and ramifications in such circumstances.

IDEALISM

It was exciting. It was stimulating. My newfound spiritual belief system blew like a fresh breeze through spring leaves in the convolutions of my mind. It gave me structure in the midst of my grasping young adulthood. I joined the church, became zealous for the cause, and soon packed my bags; off to seminary I went to prepare for the ministry. For me, the sun rose and set on my new denomination.

Then slowly, gradually, there appeared thread-sized cracks, then gaping holes in this belief system I once accepted so readily. At first it was easy to deny the cracks existed; any manifestation of the cracks had to be wrong. The staggering options began to confront me like a two-by-four placed forcefully between my eyes. I could continue my theological sidestepping, or I could admit to my new understanding. As the theological storm gathered, the castle of theological security I had built began to deteriorate rapidly. I was exposed to an increasing crisis of denominational identity. The internal turmoil was horrific.

THE BATTLE

I watched as the lines of battle were drawn. Labels such as *conservative* and *liberal* made it easier to identify who was on which side. These labels were also confusing, however, because there was no consensus about what they really meant. Slowly but surely people's loyalty to the denomination was questioned. Those attempting to hang on to the status quo were attacked for not understanding the real historical roots of the church. Those wanting change were accused of being radicals and not true members of the church. Shortly, the debate escalated far beyond words to resignations and firings. Many who had given their entire lives to the work of the church were suddenly ostracized and without church employment.

Theological navel-gazing became the favorite pastime. I found myself caught up in trivial discussions and readings. The medieval theologians who debated about how many angels could dance on the head of a pin had nothing on our attention to detail. There was a certain enticement, sometimes an addiction, in the pursuit of the answers to the theological controversy. As I now reflect upon it, this was largely unproductive.

THE DECISION

The fact is, I gradually found myself out of harmony with the beliefs of my denomination. My love affair with it kept me hanging on, but eventually the relationship could no longer be sustained. For a number of years, I sought to affirm the beliefs that I could and to keep a low profile on the issues that I could not accept or that would create too much controversy. After a while, however, this no longer seemed entirely ethical. I watched as my more outspoken friends got fired or were moved to an ecclesiastical Siberia. The spiritual crisis grew inside me until I at last decided to resign and change to another denomination. Later I wrote the following to a friend:

To put my experience in the form of a metaphor: As you know, I didn't move when a little water got into the ship. When the storm clouds gathered overhead, many were leaving then and I too was tempted, but I hung on. I didn't leave when the storm hit full force. More left then and I grew more and more frustrated. I attempted to repair where I could even though at times I too wanted to jump. However, when things got back to normal and I realized no preparations were being made for the coming of another storm, that all was back to the same old rock-a-long status quo, and nothing, not even the storm had awakened the captains and most of the sailors, I finally decided it was time to jump ship!

It was a decision made slowly and prayerfully. It was a decision I have never regretted making. However, it was a painful decision because many friends and church members felt betrayed by it and had no understanding of what I was doing. My associations with people from my seminary and with my ministerial friends would never be the same. Loss was involved because of my personal life investment in the denomination. I had to grieve, but the healing has come and I am happy with my decision.

Since those times I have come to realize that what happened to me in my small denomination is only a microcosm of a similar struggle that has occurred and is occurring in many denominations. It has characterized religious groups no matter where one looks in history or where one looks on the face of the globe. In fact, the New Testament rings of controversy. It reminds me of the short poem someone wrote: "To dwell above with saints we love, oh, that will be glory! To dwell below with saints we know, oh, that's another story!" (Perry and Shawchuck, 1982, p. 87). Part of the difficulty I suppose comes from the smorgasbord of personalities we have in our churches, part from our temptation (due to our own insecurities) to exclude those who disagree with us, part from the way institutions tend to allow the hierarchical assumptions and structures to become rigidified, part from the generalization of theological "expertise," and so on. Let's face it, none of us and no church has a monopoly on becoming unbalanced.

ACTIONS TO TAKE WHEN FACING
A DENOMINATIONAL CRISIS

From my experience and my perspective, I believe certain actions can help those confronted with a personal crisis of denominational identity, and I would like to share my reflections on these actions.

Move Slowly

In the heat of controversy one can be tempted to react too quickly and then later question if one did the right thing. It is best to allow time for processing in order to have as few regrets as possible. Unless conscience is being compromised, it is usually best to move slowly. There isn't necessarily any merit in being the first casualty in a theological turkey shoot. Be wise and careful with whom you share any newfound views. Do not cause any more agitation and conflict than is necessary.

It is also important not to reject everything because some parts are bad; all religious movements have their share of problems. It is important to assess the depth of the conflict and the potential adjustment one can make to it. Move at your own speed; let no one else dictate when you need to change a belief or leave a church. You are the one who must live with your decision.

Seek Counsel

I found it very helpful to seek out trusted persons of greater experience and discuss the issues with them. Many had the wisdom to give me a deeper insight into the issues at hand. They also helped me distinguish between the trivial and the essential. There was something about this contact with those of more experience that was a stabilizing influence in a sea of uncertainty. Many pastoral counselors can understand many of your struggles to some degree or another. Such struggles may be more common than you realize.

Explore Options

Large institutions normally change slowly, if at all. Therefore, it may well be that denominations must be left behind for ones that are more in harmony with a person's developing beliefs. On the other hand, there may be a place for you that will take you out of the theological battles (at least for a while), but that will still allow continued personal study and a challenging ministry.

Widen Perspectives

In most theological controversies extremes exist on both sides of the issues. Be careful not to go to an extreme. Your anchor may have been pulled up, and you will be adrift for a while. Moderation is a key to health, including spiritual health.

It is easy to narrow our focus in the heat of battle and lose sight of the larger teachings of the gospel. We can lose sight of the monumental teachings such as grace, gospel freedom, and love to God and humankind (even our theological enemies). We can suffer from theological myopia, blind to the larger issues. Charles Simeon wrote in 1825: "The truth is not in the middle, and not in one extreme, but in both extremes" (Carus, 1847, p. 600). This is not bad counsel to ponder in the midst of extremes. The tendency is to limit our focus to one extreme, believing we have all the "truth." Actually, in such circumstances we need a theological wide-angle lens and a wide-angle heart to take in even those with whom we disagree.

Start immediately to broaden your social network if you are isolated. It will take time, and you may not have the same comfort level initially with new social relationships as you had with the organization you are leaving. You may feel the loss of the identity you experienced with those you knew for years with whom you held a common belief system. The transition to new friendships and relationships takes time.

Another aspect of widening your perspective is to develop new interests and activities in your life. You cannot and should not study the issues all the time. Exercise and seek to find a balance in life. You will need some diversion and healthy distractions.

Allow Grief

Disappointment occurs when our belief system is challenged, changed, or possibly even collapsed. Shifting something that is or has been very important to us, and an integral or intrinsic part of our existence, cannot be done without an experience of loss. We may find ourselves with spiritual numbness, with confusion, with fear, with sadness, or with anger (see Chapter 4). There may be a questioning of more fundamental doctrines in the process. It is important that we work through this rather than stifle the process.

Keep your passion, but grieve over the loss of some of your idealism. There is no perfect religious structure. However, you will eventually find great satisfaction in being on an honest spiritual pilgrimage where you can discuss issues with integrity and openness.

Move On

If we maintain the intensity of religious controversy indefinitely we will most likely become negative people. At some point we must stop focusing on the negative and controversial and move on with our lives. It may necessitate a change of career position or denomination, but we must move on. The saddest people I witness in this area are those who have hung on to controversy so long that they are stuck in destructive thought patterns. A life should not be based on negatives. Some controversy can be stimulating and growth producing, but continued feeding on such can leave us spiritual skeletons.

Refocus

Realize anew that God is bigger and better than any religious system, and your salvation does not depend on any organizational structure. Refocus on the challenge of new ventures of faith and on how your life can be an example of the continual renewal and reformation that Christ calls us to in discipleship. Christ does not call us to the status quo, but to growth.

My own experience with a personal crisis of denominational identity was a grueling process, yet it was also a process of spiritual development. I am changed as a result. It has broadened my perspective of the church and of the Christian community. I am not so confident that I have all the doctrinal answers as I once was, but there is a certain freedom in realizing that no person and no denomination has all the answers. We are all spiritual pilgrims searching and struggling.

There is a myth in some religious systems that a person who leaves the organization will not survive spiritually or psychologically. This myth makes it more difficult for some to leave oppressive religious systems. However, this myth is truly a myth. Multitudes are enjoying the freedom of newfound ways of serving and worshiping Christ in a spirit of freedom and have overcome the psychological trauma of a toxic religious system. I am thankful to be one of them.

No church is perfect. However, I finally came to the conclusion that it is important to belong to a denomination that does not stifle my spiritual journey, but enhances it. The jungle of continual controversy and antagonism has given way to opportunities for my spiritual renewal.

QUESTIONS FOR DISCUSSION/REFLECTION

1. At what point would you leave a denomination/church, if ever?
2. What steps would you go through if you changed to another denomination/church?
3. What would be the crisis points for you with such a change?
4. What do you look for in a denomination/church to which you wish to belong?
5. How do you explain the existence of so many denominations?
6. How important is denominational identity to you?

7. How important do you think denominational identity is to most people today and do you anticipate any changes in degrees of loyalty to denominations in the future?
8. What are the major areas of conflict within your denomination?
9. How should denominations/churches seek to resolve major conflicts?
10. What inspires you about your denomination/church?

Chapter 6

When Ministry Disillusions

In recent years "compassion fatigue" has been used to describe a possible effect of working in the helping professions. A process of depleting the energy of the helper occurs over time when assisting others. This can be true whether one is an ordained minister, lay worker in the church, or simply a friend, and especially true when working with those who have been traumatized. Therefore, it is important to address this type of crisis in the life of the person helping others. This chapter presents some basic processes for restoring and replenishing the spiritual life of the minister or helper when working with people in crisis. The main theme is that regaining a balanced spirituality can make a critical difference to once-energetic counselors who are now suffering from disillusionment or burnout, and maintaining a spiritual balance can be protective for those entering the field. The present chapter and Exhibit 6.1 suggest important issues to keep in place in our lives as caregivers.

Christian spirituality offers us the ability to tap into the power of the Holy Spirit through a relationship with Christ. This relationship can help provide the needed strength to deal with the wear and tear of helping others in crisis. It gives us a resource for rest and strength that provides an oasis of peace and fortitude that we do not have by ourselves alone. In particular, a spiritual life can help one to have a greater sense of transcendence, solitude, discipline, and community.

**EXHIBIT 6.1. Important Self-Care Principles
for Caregivers**

- Keep a broad spiritual grounding and perspective.
- Practice the spiritual disciplines.
- Allow for relaxation and recreation.
- Set limits and boundaries with work.
- Acknowledge and appropriately express feelings.
- Accept support and friendships from others.
- Monitor level of exhaustion; know when to take a break.
- Practice good health habits (proper sleep, diet, and exercise).
- Spend time in self-reflection and observation.
- Have personal goals that energize.
- Know and accept limitations of helping others.
- Avoid becoming too serious; cultivate laughter.

FINDING MEANING IN LIFE

A foundational concept for working with others is transcendence, which is being able to move beyond the immediate to see the larger picture or to see greater possibilities than what we see with our natural eyes. Transcendent spirituality can help individuals find and maintain meaning in life. This purpose may be found by transcending the individual self as in the belief in God or a higher power or by descending to a place deep within each being.

Far too often counselors and helpers get caught up in the immediate crisis and fail to look at the larger issues of life. This can occur with both trained professionals and nonprofessionals who are involved with those in crisis as well as during long periods of intense assistance. Some go to the other extreme and become "so heavenly minded that they are no earthly good." Maintain a balance with this.

However, in order not to be overwhelmed, helpers need to realize the freedom to choose personal attitudes in any given situation. This is vital according to those who have been able to endure hardship and trauma and have survived well by finding a way to choose even in the midst of severe external control and abuse. This human freedom can assist helpers in transcending the limitations of the present crisis, whether personal or at the time of assisting others. It gives the individual a broader basis for finding meaning in life. Believing in the concept of God or a higher power presents a reality and meaning in life beyond the immediate senses.

Paul Tillich (1952) wrote in *The Courage to Be* that individuals need to have the courage to "live from the inside." A deep experience of transcendence can help achieve this when the pressures of life are too great. Individuals can relate differently if they are able to be in touch with the immediate situation, yet look beyond it to other potentialities.

FINDING SANCTUARY

Closely related to the concept of inner transcendence is that of solitude. Many people do not reach out until they have "hit bottom" in their lives. Many who ask for help are only beginning to face extremely stressful situations that have precipitated a crisis for them. We need a spiritual self in a relationship with Christ that provides internal solitude. If the only self we are in contact with is the self that is relating to the disastrous event or condition, it is no wonder that many in the helping fields experience burnout. We all need to have a place or a community of solitude in which we can replenish personal vitality and energy.

Such a place may be our internal relationship with Christ or it may be supplemented by something external to the personal self. Mystics and spiritual pilgrims throughout history have found retreats of solitude necessary to keep them in contact with their spirituality. These sanctuaries can be churches or temples; they can also be places that incorporate the beauty and peace of nature. For some it is a community of support, acceptance, and freedom to be oneself.

There is a spiritual quality in taking a walk in the woods when the aloneness is connected with God in nature. Just as churches may sometimes be safe and peaceful sanctuaries for church members, caregivers also need a sanctuary uninterrupted by stress and commotion to find an inner peace.

LEARN TO SURRENDER

Ministers sometimes speak of resistant people who have not learned how to surrender. However, ministers and other caregivers in the church also have this problem. Caregivers are not all-powerful and cannot help everyone solve all their problems. Some caregivers work with a messiah or Christ complex, believing they can save all people from past traumas, present problems, and future difficulties. We are not Christ or the Messiah. It is important to be optimistic, but also to be realistic. We may be an instrument of "salvation," but salvation does not come from us.

It is detrimental when caregivers adjust and deal with some of their messiah complex yet continue to believe that they alone have the ability to get others to change. This can cause burnout because caregivers fall into the trap of codependency. In other words, caregivers can begin to base their worth on the success or failure of the person whom they are helping. Thus each time the person fails, the caregiver feels like a failure. Even in the church, caregivers can get caught up in a results- and goal-driven agenda that keeps them on edge and dissatisfied. It can help keep them on track to realize that their job is not to reap the harvest, but to sow the seed.

A SENSE OF DISCIPLINE

Too often today we ignore the discipline involved in spirituality. There is a danger when we simply lump everything into the concept of spirituality. One of the misuses of the term *spirituality* today may be the neglect of the disciplines that have historically been associated with the spiritual. Some aspects of spirituality do not occur without a disciplined focus and/or a trained grounding for our lives.

Balanced spirituality requires some form of discipline, even if it is simply scheduling a walk with God in nature. It also requires discipline to find the inner self and to transcend the limits of the present situation. Many have incorporated some type of "centering" or meditation as a spiritual discipline. Meditation can be defined as listening to God and to ourselves. The discipline would not be in the working at it; it would be in the surrender to it. Rather than thinking of the split between the psyche and the body (soma) that is so common in Western thought, we should think of a "wholeness" in which being in touch with the inner self is being in touch with the whole being. This may include the need for a more balanced diet, proper exercise, and more rest.

Christian caregivers also need to be disciplined by having other interests besides the church and reading about theology or even the Bible. A narrow focus on life does not take into consideration the vastness of the spiritual being. Discipline that aids counselors in addressing the whole being can be a very important safeguard against compassion fatigue.

INCORPORATING OTHERS

Many Christian caregivers are both lonely and alone. This may be a danger of many in the helping professions. A minister who was feeling burnout wrote the following in a paper for a class I taught: "Ministers generally feel a great deal of loneliness. We get little support or encouragement. Many of us reach a point where there is nothing left to give." It is no longer a secret that many believe that ministry has had a negative impact on their personal and family lives. There is often an unrealistic pressure from the congregation or from inside the minister to be the ideal person or have the ideal family. This pressure leads to a facade that prevents sharing of the clergyperson's own pains and struggles and isolates the minister even more. Similar issues can hamper lay leaders in the church.

An unbalanced relationship can exist when caregivers share very little about themselves while the people they are assisting pour out the deepest pains of their souls. While expected and normal at times, all our relationships should not have this pattern. Being a caregiver can be an escape for some as they live vicariously through the feelings of others while avoiding personal issues. It can be a disaster if caregivers use their caregiving to escape personal feelings and relationships with others.

Christian caregivers must be in community and in relationship with others outside those they assist. As spiritual beings, individuals need to belong to a community because it can magnify happiness and lessen pain. Several models of ministries emphasize this need, yet often caregivers fail to recognize their own denied needs. Finding a place to belong, to be in real community, and to experience connectedness should be a high priority for those in helping positions.

Spirituality added to the caregiver's personal life can mean the difference between finding purpose and satisfaction in helping or becoming a casualty to compassion fatigue. Therefore, attention to the caregiver's own spirituality may lessen the potential of becoming disappointed with the church. Sometimes the depletion from unbalanced ways of caring adds to our frustration with the church. Caregivers need to look at the needs of their own spiritual and personal lives as clearly as they have learned to look at the needs of those they are assisting.

QUESTIONS FOR DISCUSSION/REFLECTION

1. Are only certain personality types called to be caregivers?
2. What do you think of the term *compassion fatigue?* Is it a valid term for those who are called to minister to others?
3. How can one transcend the immediate crisis and be in touch with a sanctuary within?
4. In what places or in what ways do you find peace and rest?
5. How do you define *messiah complex?*
6. Do you think it is possible to get too busy doing the work of God?
7. Why do so many ministers burn out? What could your church do to be more emotionally supportive of your minister(s)?
8. Do you think the expectations for ministers and church leaders make it difficult for them to be real and genuine before others?
9. How would you describe your concept of the ideal minister?
10. How would you describe your concept of the ideal congregation?

Chapter 7

When Tensions Increase

First Church of "My Way or No Way" was involved in explosive conflict. The church was dividing like two opposing army camps, hunkering down and digging in their heels. One group was compiling all the biblical verses about moving forward in faith while the other was collecting all the verses about being wise stewards.

The issue at hand was whether to build a new sanctuary. Some thought the church needed to move by faith and build to accommodate more new members from the growing community nearby. Others felt sure that God had called the church to exhibit wise stewardship and live within its means. There was little more than seed money for the new sanctuary, and the second group believed that most of the money for the building should be raised before the project was begun. "We teach our children about responsible use of money and living within their means, so how can we ignore this principle as a church?" they repeatedly argued. The other group countered, "God wants us to depend on Him. When we are doing His will, He will provide the financial means." The debate was moving beyond discussion to personal verbal attacks between the two groups. Meanwhile, down on the next corner, First Church of "We Are Right and They Are Wrong" was having its own struggles.

The suggestion of this chapter is that truth has many sides; many conflicts in the church occur because some members focus on one aspect of the truth while others focus on another. This can precipitate many misunderstandings and disappointments within the church. Whether we are theologically liberal or conservative, we can become unbalanced and focus on one aspect of reality to the neglect of other parts.

Whole denominations and movements have been built on one belief to the neglect of others. Entire lives have been lived concentrating on one side of a belief. Klyne Snodgrass (1990), in his book *Between Two Truths,* presents the following story that illustrates this well:

> Once the Devil was walking along with one of his cohorts. They saw a man ahead of them pick up something shiny. "What did he find?" asked the cohort. "A piece of the truth," the Devil replied. "Doesn't that bother you that he found a piece of the truth?" asked the cohort. "No," said the Devil, "I will see to it that he makes a religion out of it." (p. 35)

"We are right and they are wrong" is a common stance taken, sometimes openly, at other times behind the scenes. Therefore, more and more attention is given to the one side or part of a belief to prove that it is correct. This gives a certain sense of security and self-righteousness, but often at a tremendous cost.

A NARROW FOCUS
RESULTS IN LACK OF TOLERANCE

Following one line of thinking usually blinds us to the other side and brings forth intolerance for the contradicting view. To admit or acknowledge any of the opposite side as true begins to crack our security about being right and increases our anxiety that we might even be wrong. We thus filter out of our lives what doesn't immediately fit with our belief and focus on only what can be explained by our belief structure. A strategy of conflict, instead of a dialogue-based approach, is thus set up with those who see things differently. When we do this we try to impose our view and thus develop one way of thinking or acting and support it. This prevents openness to change even when someone may present clear evidence of another aspect of the belief.

NOT ACCEPTING TENSIONS RESULTS IN LACK OF CHALLENGE

This method of thinking and living impacts us by removing certain challenges from our lives, thus resulting in a lack of growth. We no longer allow ourselves to be challenged by the ambiguities and difficulties of life. Although we may have an uneasy feeling of being challenged by the other aspects of a belief, we usually keep this as far away from consciousness as possible. We are comfortable in our ways of thinking and are not willing to step outside of our own comfort zone.

Living on one side of a belief keeps us from hearing and processing the other aspects of the truth. We need to be flexible enough to step outside our comfort zone and struggle with additional aspects of truth. Otherwise we will view life and conflicts as inflexible categories of good/bad, white/black, or either/or. Our options and possibilities thus become narrowed with tunnel vision. Many have been disappointed with their experience in the church because members have become inflexible. As we struggle with integration we don't have to force-fit life and thinking into a particular mode. We can better live with tensions, contradictions, and ambiguities.

Living with polarities can assist us in accepting the contradictions within ourselves by normalizing them. We can, therefore, better acknowledge our hate as well as our love, our selfishness as well as our altruism, and our evil as well as our good. We can better embrace our "shadow side," as Carl Jung called it, rather than denying its existence or projecting it onto others. This can result in better dealing with our conflicting emotions about others, as well as conflicting emotions within us. Processing can occur when we listen to the conflicts inside of ourselves. Synthesis of opposing forces or thoughts is a means of growth and is motivationally enhancing because it brings us to a new understanding.

INTEGRATION RESULTS IN MORE BALANCE

Integration of polarities makes us less eager to propose we have the final answer and more open to the possibility of hearing the beliefs of others. Integration gives us a greater appreciation for the diversity of understandings and interpretations in life and belief. The resulting willingness to be more inclusive opens us to being taught the limitations of the aspects of life we might be denying or ignoring.

This doesn't mean we do not debate and have firm convictions, but in the midst of our convictions we can continue to hear what opposing people are stating. None of us do this perfectly, but an integrative approach to beliefs assists us in being less relationally dogmatic. It also assists us in moving back and forth as needed, depending on the situation. Noel Mason (1982) wrote in an editorial for *Good News Unlimited*:

> Every Christian community . . . needs a conservative like James and a progressive like Paul. The church must learn to live in the tension between the old and the new, between the vision and the revision, form and reform. We can't travel very far in a car that only has a brake, and who would risk driving in one that only had an accelerator? There are times in any journey when a motorist needs both to survive. (p. 2)

POLARITIES IN THE CHRISTIAN LIFE

Snodgrass (1990) with wise insight stated the following about polarities in the Christian faith:

Tension permeates our faith. Every truth that we know is balanced by another truth that seems to be moving in the opposite direction. . . . Our faith is lived out between two or more competing truths, neither of which may be relinquished. We live between truths. . . . We do not like complexity and tension. In fact, in order to keep life simple we will suppress those things that hint at complexities. We accept partial truths, stereotypes, and generalizations, even if they do not fit the facts. . . . Our attempts to make life and faith simple derives from our need to find some handle by which to control the complexity around us. (p. 28)

Some of the polarities in the Christian life follow:

- Faith versus works
- Law versus grace
- Sinner versus saint
- Submission versus authority
- Divine versus human
- Time versus eternity

Several of these are discussed by Snodgrass (1990) and are familiar once we pause to consider them. An illustration he gives is helpful when thinking about tension or polarities in the Christian life:

Tension in the Christian life is not like a tightrope where we must fear falling off either side. There would be no peace in that. A more appropriate image is that of a stringed instrument. Properly attached at the two right places, the instrument can be played. If a string is left too loose, music cannot be produced. If it is stretched too tightly, the string will break. (p. 32)

Snodgrass gives these guidelines to help us with polarity thinking: First of all, we need to practice holistic thinking, which begins by recognizing our own incompleteness and by being open to people of differing perspectives. Holistic thinking will help us question the limitations of statements and opinions. Second, we must allow for unity and diversity within the church. The recognition of our incompleteness will require both unity and diversity as we seek to gain the perspective of those who are different from us. Snodgrass cautions that unity is not uniformity and diversity is not division. A third guideline is to accept our humanity. To be human is to have to deal with polarity, tension, confusion, incompleteness, and limited understanding.

Thus the tensions of the Christian life are important struggles we should not avoid, but should accept as part of the journey. We must deal with complexity if we are to live in reality. Church members who do this will lessen their potential conflict and disillusionment with the church.

QUESTIONS FOR DISCUSSION/REFLECTION

1. When in life is a person more likely to go to extremes?
2. Have you known people or organizations who appeared to be oriented to one side of an extreme?
3. What have been your own struggles with going to an extreme?
4. Are there any preventive measures to keep us from extremes?
5. How do you counsel a person whom you think to be extreme?
6. How do we find balance in life?
7. Can you think of biblical characters who were extremist?
8. How is the concept of spiritual gifts related to this topic of balance in life?

9. Do you think we live very well with tensions (various theological beliefs, for example) in the church?
10. Are debate and disagreement healthy for the church? Are we uncomfortable with these two avenues of sharing?

Chapter 8
When Change Collides

First Church of "The Pastor Is the Problem" of Stuckville just fired another pastor. The church has had seven pastors in the past ten years. Some ministers chose to leave before they were fired; others fought to the bitter end, but were dismissed by vote of the board and then of the church. The church leaders are quick to discuss the deplorable state of the pool of eligible clergy candidates. "Pastors just aren't what they used to be," was the statement of one elder. Church members expect the pastor to visit them on a weekly basis just as was done by their beloved minister who served them for ten years a few decades ago.

The congregation demands that the traditional yearly revival with all its standard songs be maintained. Even with the changing demographics in the area and the many young professionals in the neighborhood, no new members have joined the church in seven years. Visitors sometimes come, but they just don't return. The church members do not understand why their membership is declining. "We are presenting the same message in the same way that worked in the past." A strong suspicion exists that ministers are out of touch with the needs of the church and this is seen as the reason for the struggles of the church. The church members point to their willingness to experience the pain of changing ministers as evidence that they are open to change, even when it hurts.

CONCEPTS ABOUT CHANGE

Family systems theory includes the ideas of first and second order change or what we might call real change versus superficial change. Superficial change is basically moving things around without really changing the system. An example might be the exit from a family of a child who is in a certain role and the next child in line taking up the same role after the older child leaves. A child who has been the scapegoat or black sheep of the family may leave, and the next child then becomes the focus of the tension in the family. Another example is the family that stops fighting about one issue only to focus their anger on another issue. The family system basically remains the same. Superficial change is similar to the popular statement about rearranging the chairs on the *Titanic* as it was going down. Energy is expended, but does not address the problematic issue. Real change necessitates a restructuring change of the family system. The family described previously would change its organization instead of passing the role along, thus addressing the family tension in a new way.

CHANGE AND CHURCHES

I would like to apply these concepts to churches. Some churches operate with a superficial change mentality in which the same theology is repeated over and over. The same people maintain leadership roles. I read of one church that had the same Sunday school superintendent for forty-seven years. It may have been that the person was very good at the position, but I would tend to bet that not much new energy came into the Sunday school with the same person holding the position for so long. The only solutions to problems that are tried are the ones that have been tried previously. Not all of this is bad or dysfunctional, but if a church gets locked into this pattern it loses many of its opportunities.

Some churches maintain stability, but also incorporate real changes as necessary. Members respond to new developments and to the new needs of individuals and the community. They find new ways to express old truths. They are open to changing the organization of the church if it enhances their mission. They are more interested in people than in programs, activities for show, or just keeping the machinery running, so to speak. They are involved in the real world with real people. I believe such a church is what most of us desire today.

At an organizational level, many of the issues that disillusion members occur because the church is stuck in superficial change that doesn't adapt to new situations. Many see the church operating in the same manner it did in the past, and that manner is no longer relevant for them. If they have not been raised in the church, the language used by the church may be incomprehensible. It no longer speaks to their hearts and no longer confronts the issues of their lives. The message may have truth, but it is old wine in old wineskins. Churches need new wine in new wineskins.

Of course, real change in the church can also create disillusionment. Some members are threatened by new ways of doing things. Those who are stuck with more and more of the same don't appreciate change. Sometimes, however, we all need to be shaken out of our complacency. Christianity is a "real change" religion, and to limit it to "superficial impact" religion destroys its power. When the church becomes the institution of the status quo it loses the creative energy of the spirit. We need a balance between change and stability, tradition and innovation, ritual and spontaneity.

SUPERFICIAL CHANGE

In sociology, the concept of cultural lag basically states that cultures continue to socialize their members to patterns of behavior long after those patterns have ceased to be relevant to a society's survival. Unfortunately, many of our churches are experiencing a profound cultural lag. Disappointment occurs when the church does not address current issues. Some churches are speaking to the issues of generations ago, not to the generation of today.

Many churches simply do not know what to do or how to get moving in the right direction. Church members, like everyone else, have many responsibilities pulling at their lives and may not have the energy for working out all the difficulties of the church. However, far too often more energy is spent maintaining the status quo than would be spent by allowing for creative change to occur.

This model of the church as being stuck at superficial change can be illustrated by several biblical stories, such as an adaptation of the popular parable of the prodigal son. When the younger son left the church, he joined more progressive institutions and began partying without limits. He ended up destitute and realized that ultimately the church did have something to offer. He then decided to return to the church and sit in the pews and worship. The great love and acceptance of God has penetrated his indifference. He is undergoing a real change of heart as he has come to recognize his great need. Upon his return to the church, he is welcomed by the members who recognize the need for grace in their lives and in the lives of others. They welcomed the "backslider" with open arms and even threw a party to celebrate his return. There were some in the church, however, who were not so pleased. They didn't see any exceptions to the tried-and-true way of church organization and activity. These elder brothers and sisters were angry and bitter about this backslider receiving so much attention and being given a party in the church. They had been faithfully doing the duties of the church and had not been recognized, so why should this unfaithful person be recognized even if he has returned? The backslider might bring new ideas into the church from the world. This had never been done before and the older members spurned this new way of accepting others.

Another story concerns the woman caught in adultery. The crowd pushed and shoved her in front of Jesus, all eyes riveted on her. The voices of the church members were akin to a hunter who has just made a big kill. Like moral vultures they have been trained to rip the sinner to pieces. They fully expect Jesus to condemn her to death. They at least were attempting to trap him into this. The agony of the woman did not concern them. They were tied into a legalist approach and were following what they had been taught. They were stuck in keeping the letter of the law without its spirit and purpose of being helpful to people. Jesus turned their thinking upside down. Rather than condemning her again and repeating the law she has broken (the superficial approach because the woman has heard it before), he showed her true compassion. She left with a heart much more impacted and changed than would have occurred with the treatment of the church members. Real change changes hearts.

Another example is the Pharisees to whom Jesus spoke harshly. He said they did not practice what they preached and placed heavy demands on the people that they did not place on themselves. Jesus condemned their hypocrisy and their neglect of the important issues of justice, mercy, and faithfulness. At one point he said to these religious rulers: "Woe to you, teachers of the law and Pharisees, you hypocrites! You are like whitewashed tombs, which look beautiful on the outside but on the inside are full of dead men's bones and everything unclean. In the same way, on the outside you appear to people as righteous but on the inside you are full of hypocrisy and wickedness" (Matthew 23:27-28). The Pharisees were promoting religious conformity and ritual without having any real change that impacted their hearts at a deeper level.

CHANGE NEVER COMES EASILY

Lest we be too hard on the people in the examples in the previous section, think of how difficult real change is for most of us. After listening for thousands of hours to people in psychotherapy I have come to the conclusion that most of us do not change very easily. For many of us it takes a crisis to bring about actions that cause change.

It becomes even more difficult to speak of change as we move from individuals to groups to institutions. Institutions do not change very quickly; that is one reason they are called institutions. By definition, an institution is an established way of being or doing. Churches are some of the slower institutions to change because so many religious, traditional, cultural, and individual factors are involved. Lest we be too critical of the religious institutions, just pause to think of government or educational institutions and how slowly they move until a crisis motivates change.

THE CHURCH: A PROJECTION OF US?

I have alluded to parts that we may sometimes play in our disillusionment with the church. However, I have basically described ways the church experiences problems from the viewpoint of a detached observer. Briefly, I would like to focus more closely on how we personally may contribute to this problem of disillusionment. I have already noted the unrealistic expectations we sometimes have with the church. It may be important for us to examine the projections we place on the church. Are the issues that disappoint us ones that we project and blame when we see them in the church but ignore in ourselves?

Unwanted parts of us may be easier to fight if they are in the church rather than only in ourselves. It is far too easy to expect the church to be totally accepting of us while we are not very accepting of the church. It is easy to be perfectionistic and allow little grace for the church while expecting the church to be gracious to us. The human tendency is to want the church to minister to our every need while we do not minister to others in the church with needs. We can project our expectations that the church should be growing and developing while we are stagnant and complacent. We project our need for change onto the institution while we protect our "comfort zones" and ourselves.

WHEN CHANGE AND CHURCH COLLIDE

Most churches are based on a mentality several decades old, if not older. This has not caused much difficulty in the past because many sections of the country were culturally similar and societal change was relatively slow. However, with the advent of television and then the Internet, the diversity of the world is coming into our households. New and different perspectives challenge the traditional ways of thinking and behaving. The generation gap continues to widen the gulf between how parents thought as teenagers and how their children think as teenagers.

Therefore, enormous challenges face any institution that attempts to reach across the life cycle. The church seeks to minister to all people at all stages of life, mainly from the same worship service. Not an easy feat to begin with, but when combined with slow adaptability to change this becomes almost impossible. Thus it is reasonable to have some sympathy for the church and the challenges before it. The church should not always be the first to make new changes, but neither should it be the last to change.

Without change, many churches will gradually cease to function. Smaller churches are currently having great difficulty supporting a minister and paying their bills. A growing number of people want a church that can provide choices, services, and activities that small churches cannot support. In past generations the same community has been able to support numerous small churches of various denominations. Somehow these small churches may need to unite if they are to survive in any functional way.

The commitment of years past, in which members would continue to feel an obligation to the church despite dull services, is slipping away. Although persons today are willing to be committed, they are not content to support a church that has little relevance to them.

Another change to which the church must adapt is that the hierarchical structure of some religious organizations is no longer accepted. Many will not follow instructions or legislations sent down from authorities distant to them. They want to see the local manifestation of their efforts and have more control regarding use of their pledges.

These are just a few of the many earthquakes shaking the church today. Change is here and is increasing. The church cannot survive if it continues to be like a horse and buggy driving down the interstate. Society will pass it by and eventually relegate it to the back roads. The church must be innovative and creative and seek real change with depth.

THE OPPORTUNITY

Fortunately, with the crisis comes the opportunity for great movement. As stated previously, I believe that individuals and institutions normally do not change effectively unless motivated by crisis. The motivation to change at an institutional level can build so gradually that the institution dies before real change occurs. However, some signs of movement have appeared in the church, as people seek more depth in their personal faith and ministry activities. The church can become a tool for expression of this new spiritual interest. Thus there is hope for the church if true change can be allowed to permeate its structure and message.

Some who are disillusioned with the church have grasped the need for changes and have attempted to implement them. The resistance they have encountered has caused them to lose hope. Understanding the dynamics of institutions and the difficulty of change can help them in rethinking the process. Yet we need their dissatisfaction to push us toward the changes that are critical for religious organizations. In the church we have been too quick to dismiss those who perturb and disturb us, and perhaps those who perturb and disturb us have, at times, given up on the church too quickly. Change is a constant of life, therefore, the church must accept it as a reality and find appropriate ways to incorporate change. Such change needs to occur at a pace that isn't too impulsive, yet is not so slow that the church becomes a fossil.

QUESTIONS FOR REFLECTION/DISCUSSION

1. When a church has many pastors within a short number of years, what are the possible dynamics?
2. What are some examples of superficial changes that churches make?
3. What are some example of churches that have made significant changes?
4. How do churches change in a positive manner?
5. What are some of the issues that changes raise?
6. Is the church keeping pace with needed changes?
7. How is the church a projection of us? How can this be a factor for change or a resistance to change?
8. What are some potential directions for change the church should take?
9. How does the church keep its loyalty to the past and accept the present?
10. How does the church change in ways similar to those of other institutions? How does it change differently?

Chapter 9

When Humanity Fails

Many of us believe that physical health checkups are an important part of our health maintenance. Checkups can alert us to potential avoidable physical crises: "Mr. Smith, your blood pressure is high. I'm going to give you some medication to help control it." Checkups can also encourage us to move in a more positive direction: "Mr. Smith, you are a bit overweight. Have you thought about losing a few pounds?" Some of the problems found during a checkup, such as high blood pressure, may surprise us. We may be too aware of other problems such as being overweight, but need a little coaching to make positive changes.

The church may also need a checkup from time to time to assess how members are doing and to avoid potential crises. Unhealthy ways of thinking and being can lead us down the road to an eventual spiritual or emotional crisis. Unfortunately, distorted ways of thinking and being are often found in the church. Sometimes members even use the church and theology for the manifestation of sick psychological and relational behaviors. This chapter briefly outlines some of the unhealthy beliefs and behaviors that can lead to disappointment in the church.

THE CRISIS OF POLLYANNA DELUSIONS: DENIAL

One of the most prevalent crises is that of Pollyanna delusions. Some people and families have a powerful dynamic that they always must say everything is fine. They must deny everything bad or negative. Although it is important to think of the positive, as the apostle Paul says, "Whatever is true . . . think on these things," we must also be realistic and not blind to situations that need to be addressed.

People should seek balance in their temperaments and optimism/ pessimism tendencies. An unrealistic optimism that too often uses denial may set us up for disappointment. There is a parable about twin brothers who are exactly alike except that one was eternally optimistic and the other always pessimistic. The parents decided to test the extent of the pessimism and optimism of their twins. They bought a large box of toys and put it in the room of the twin who was always pessimistic and bought a large box of manure and put it in the room of the optimist. They took the boys to their rooms and left them there to find the respective boxes that had been left for them. After a period of time the parents went to the room of the pessimistic twin to see how the box of toys had affected him. They opened the door and were surprised to find the little fellow sitting in the middle of the floor crying and sobbing heavily. When the parents inquired what was the matter, their son replied that these were all new toys and someday they would be broken and have to be thrown out. They comforted this son who always looked on the negative side and then checked on the son who had the box of manure placed in his room. To their surprise when they opened the door manure was being thrown all over the place as the little boy was digging furiously in the box. He was thrilled and with excitement said to his parents, "With all this manure there has to be a pony in here someplace!" Obviously, this little fellow was setting himself up for a disappointment.

We all use denial as a defense mechanism sometimes, and this can be a very important part of good mental health; some, however, push it to an extreme. Denial becomes a way of avoiding the difficulties and realities of life. It is a setup for a major fall or spiritual earthquake. One way we do this is by believing that if we live right or pray enough or have enough faith, nothing bad will happen to us. A healthy assurance about life comes from faith and trusting in God. However, when this becomes a way of ignoring the perplexities, contradictions, and ambiguities of life, it may no longer be a sign of health.

When this extreme denial is finally penetrated by a crisis or by the long-time wear and tear of life, a spiritual crisis can occur as well. It may be a prime time to fall prey to self-blame for not having prayed enough, lived close enough to God, or had enough faith. This on top of the current crisis can send the person into deep despair. It is much better to realize and confront the fact that life is not fair, just, or always good for the person of belief or anyone else. The Pollyanna attitude can be an escape from difficulties and therefore an escape from growth.

THE CRISIS OF PROJECTION: THE DEVIL MADE ME DO IT

James Framo (1981), a pioneer in the field of marriage and family therapy, has written about couple relationships in which we often project the unwanted parts of ourselves onto our mates and then fight them in our mates. We all have parts of ourselves that are difficult for us to acknowledge, admit, or bring into our awareness.

Christ confronted this idea with the words, "You hypocrite, first take the plank out of your own eye, and then you will see clearly to remove the speck from your brother's eye" (Matthew 7:5). This crisis of projection is rampant in some churches, with criticism running wild in the aisles. Sometimes it falls under the critical or mean-spirited approach; other times it goes under the banners of "the devil made me do it" or "the devil is making them do it."

Often people are most intensely critical of the behavior of others because they unconsciously desire to participate in the behavior themselves. Projection is the defense mechanism that gives our unwanted and unacceptable motives or desires to another. It can keep the focus off our own internal conflict and for a time keeps us feeling better about ourselves.

The projection of blame for our behaviors onto others is not only a characteristic of children; adults play this game also. Adam blamed Eve; Eve blamed the serpent. We do not like to admit to our own failures, betrayals, and sins. This also tends to get into an us/them approach, which has often been a destructive force in churches. Healing cannot occur while we ignore our own need for healing and/or correction.

THE CRISIS OF EXTERNAL LOCUS OF CONTROL: EXPECTING GOD TO DO IT ALL

Another personal spiritual crisis is on the horizon when people expect God or someone else to do it all. This expectation causes us to feel that we are at the fate of forces beyond our control. Although there is truth in this, it is certainly not the whole truth. In most circumstances something can be changed, influenced, or mastered. Some people have been able to feel in control of some internal aspect of their lives in the midst of terrible surroundings.

Often people who have an external locus of control become pessimists. They tend to believe the worst and to look for the bad to happen. Martin Seligman (1990) in his book *Learned Optimism* points out that the basis of pessimism is helplessness, which occurs when people believe that nothing they do can affect what happens to them. He states:

Twenty-five years of study has convinced me that if we *habitually* believe, as does the pessimist, that misfortune is our fault, is enduring, and will undermine everything we do, more of it will befall us than if we believe otherwise. I am also convinced that if we are in the grip of this view, we will get depressed more easily, we will accomplish less than our potential, and we will even get physically sick more often. Pessimistic prophecies are self-fulfilling. (p. 7)

I have had clients who have confirmed this to me again and again. Joe was very suicidal when I started working with him. Suicide was functional for him in that when in a bind he planned to commit suicide and then he was able to have a carefree attitude about life. He continually felt that nothing he could do would change the course of his life. Then he set about activating this self-fulfilling prophecy by not planning for life, but by reacting to it. The only control he initially could feel was in planning his own suicide.

When we feel that life is totally uninfluenced by us, we feel like pawns moved about by the hand of wrath, fate, or circumstances. Many who feel this way were terribly controlled as children, and as a result believe they can choose nothing for themselves as adults.

Another take on this is the belief that everything is up to God. God is expected to do everything for us: "If I don't get a job, God didn't want me to have it even though I didn't go to the interview! When God wants my life to end, He will end it; it doesn't matter if I attempt to take care of my health or not." This can set up an apathetic approach to life as well as an eventual crisis of anger and blaming God for what doesn't work out well in our lives.

My parents have a worldview that comes from their religious faith that I viewed as simplistic for a long time. It parallels to some extent Romans 8:28: "And we know that in all things God works for the good of those who love him." They believe that situations will work themselves out, eventually. This usually works in reality! For most things do work out. We cannot, however, always sit back and expect someone else to rescue us. We must participate in the plan and the action.

THE CRISIS OF LEGALISM: CONTROL

The great destroyer of happiness for many people of faith has been legalism. Legalism is a religion of human achievement. I like the way part of the first chapter of Galatians is interpreted by Wesley Nelson (1974) in his book *Liberation*:

> True liberation is an act of God. It is the exact opposite of all our struggles to achieve freedom by a show of superior strength . . . he [Christ] is not on the side of the enslavement that prevails among both the moral and immoral people when they seek to earn their acceptance by conforming to approved patterns of conduct. (pp. 1, 7)

Legalism initially gives people a pseudo feeling of being in control by performing accomplishments. It gives the feeling of being correct or righteous. This doesn't last long, however, for a greater demand always comes over the horizon and beckons conformity. We strive to "do" to be accepted by others or by God. Our world revolves around performance of duty. We are attempting to feel secure by being in control and doing all the right things.

Often this leads us to criticize others so that we appear better and therefore we feel better about ourselves. The good feeling from being "holier" than others, however, doesn't last. The other dead-end route of legalism is ultimate despair. Once we realize that we cannot always perform perfectly and that we will make mistakes in life, our basis for acceptance is shattered.

THE CRISIS OF INSTABILITY AND INSECURITY: ANXIETY

Many events in life can disrupt our view of how the world should operate, and this disruption can throw us into a crisis of instability and insecurity. Anxiety is the emotional disorder of our time. It is one of the most frequent responses of our lives. It causes us to be fearful and apprehensive. I have had clients tell me, "I live with an overriding feeling of fear in my life." Anxiety may even involve obsessions and compulsions. Religious rituals may be used as an expression of these obsessions and compulsions. This can be handicapping and incapacitating.

Although persons with severe anxiety disorders may require medication, some of the more positive statements of Christ such as, "Therefore, don't worry about tomorrow, for tomorrow will worry about itself" and "surely I am with you always" actually are similar to cognitive therapy, the most common therapy used to deal with anxiety. Cognitive approaches assist in interrupting negative thoughts. They also examine core beliefs or schemes. A core belief is a belief we have about ourselves or about the world that is an integral part of us. It may be one such as: "Something bad is going to happen." Such beliefs influence our reactions and our interpretations of events. When our core beliefs are anxiety producing, it is difficult to find rest and contentment. We may need to challenge the dominant messages and beliefs that are being promoted by the news media or our society. We cannot ignore the problems of the world, but if we focus on problems and tensions too much we will become anxious. There is bad in the world, but the other side of the picture is that there is much that is good and beautiful as well. It appears to me that we must put our primary focus on the good and not the evil of life.

Anxiety robs us of our peace. Our very fast-paced, overstimulated existence with its lack of emphasis on meditation, prayer, and communion contributes to our tenseness. Anxiety may be a message that we need to slow down and focus on what really matters or to address issues we have been neglecting in our personal and spiritual lives. Avoiding the message that anxiety is trying to give us may lead to a serious crisis in our lives.

THE CRISIS OF THE INFLATED SELF: NARCISSISM

The personality ailment called *narcissistic personality disorder* is the extreme of the inflated self and is resistant to change. Some have an inflated self that is more easily addressed. Once I had a couple in therapy, and the man said before he realized what he had said, "She loves me and so do I." He was not speaking of a healthy appreciation and love of self, but of being in love with himself. We all need to love ourselves, and Christ said, "Love your neighbor as you love yourself," indicating that self-love can be healthy. However, what we are talking about here can be destructive to self and to relationships.

We find in the biblical story of Adam and Eve a reference to them wanting to be as God, which was the first step to their downfall. According to Wayne Oates (1987) in his book *Behind the Masks,* they wanted to "be as God, totally self-contained, self-sufficient, and needing no one and nothing from anyone. . . . The cryptic thread of narcissism runs through all our natures" (p. 43). A narcissistic person in one of my churches made up his own loose standards of behavior for himself while believing that much more rigid standards should be imposed on others. He was above the rules. According to his self-report, he had an extra special connection to God. Although most, hopefully, do not go to this extreme, many of us do have some of this inflated sense of ourselves. This can set us up for a huge downfall, as has especially happened to many religious leaders who made special exceptions for their wrong behaviors. We all need the accountability of a caring and loving community that has the fortitude to challenge us when we push the limits too far.

The inflated self usually masks a very insecure self, a self that feels very inadequate and unaccepted. The inflation is a way to temporarily avoid dealing with these very painful feelings. It is best to deal with the realities of our feelings and thoughts with trusted friends who can assist us in walking through them.

THE CRISIS OF CONDEMNATION: GUILT

Some of the most troubled people are disturbed by guilt. Many are living with self-condemnation from past acts. Others suffer from an oversensitive conscience that emotionally beats them up over every imagined imperfection. Churches have for centuries used guilt as a means of motivation and control. This has wreaked havoc and destruction in many lives. Guilt feelings can stifle human relationships, feelings of self-worth, and emotional health and growth. Guilt feelings are valid when we have truly done wrong. However, the confusion comes when people judge themselves wrong when they actually have no objective guilt. Alternatively, others have continually disregarded their values to the point that the signal of guilt is no longer felt. They resemble the person who has no pain sensors, no signal to stop or change behavior.

Bruce Narramore (1984), in his book *No Condemnation,* notes the similarities and differences between the guilt we feel before God and the guilt we feel when we fail to meet the standards or expectations of others (or ourselves). Either process can result in guilt feelings. He emphasizes how important it is to distinguish between objective guilt (true guilt for wrongs done) and guilt feelings (which may be imposed by ourselves or others and not the result of actual wrongs). It is important to realize that there can be valid or invalid guilt before God and others. The conscience is not always perfect and has to be heard along with counsel and dialogue in community with others.

THE CRISIS OF CONFORMITY: MINDLESSNESS

Ellen Langer (1989), in her book *Mindfulness,* describes mindlessness as a psychological roadblock that causes us to become like automatons trapped in old mind-sets. She discusses how mind-sets that form rigid attitudes and opinions limit our choices;

our thoughts are filtered by the mind-set and either forced to fit that particular way of thinking or rejected.

Mindlessness and its resulting conformity run rampant in some church circles. Members do not think much for themselves and do not question the truthfulness of what they are told by religious leaders. "If the preacher said it, it must be from God," is the philosophy of people who let their minds become lazy.

We find parallels in the scriptures to mindlessness. Many of the religious of Jesus' day could not venture outside of their usual thinking patterns. Even when Jesus used the teaching method of parables to attempt to get around some of their restricted hearing, often it didn't work.

In her book, Langer gives some of the potential problems of mindlessness:

- A narrow self-image
- Self-induced dependence
- Compartmentalization of uncomfortable thoughts
- Loss of control
- Learned helplessness
- Stunted potential

Langer calls the opposite of mindlessness "mindfulness," which involves the ability to look at issues with openness and to see varying points of view. None of us is completely mindful, and this is also true in the church. This can be a set-up for many personal crises, including leaving us more susceptible to those who would abuse their power.

THE USE OF SPIRITUALITY AND RELIGION IN PSYCHOLOGICALLY HEALTHY WAYS

As mentioned at the beginning of this chapter, psychologically unhealthy people often use spirituality and religion in unhealthy ways. However, spirituality and religion, when appropriate, can be healthy psychological components of life. Wayne Oates (1978), in his book *The Religious Care of the Psychiatric Patient,* identifies several characteristics of this:

1. Comprehensiveness or the ability to maintain relationships with people who have different opinions and beliefs (which I think also includes being open to the various aspects of living and not limiting our perspective to one area of life)
2. A curiosity about what one does not know (including a willingness to learn and grow)
3. Ambiguity tolerance or the ability to tolerate the "many-colored spectrums of truth"
4. A sense of humor (which assists us in not taking everything too seriously and gives us the ability to laugh at ourselves)
5. Graduation (which he defines as healthy growth from one level of faith to another without the prior being totally rejected or disowned) (pp. 227, 233)

In addition, Oates maintains that in a healthy religion some understanding of suffering promotes the constants of community, hope, basic trust, and curiosity.

Xavier (1987), in a book titled *The Two Faces of Religion,* lists the characteristics of mature spirituality as authenticity, compassion, responsibility, discipline, self-respect, realistic sense of guilt, and cooperative/creative approaches in relationships. He describes the dynamic factors of mature spirituality as courage, love, and wisdom, which he believes are interconnected.

Psychological disturbance can be closely linked with a distortion of spirituality and religion. However, I want to balance this statement with my belief that psychological health is often closely linked with a proper relationship with spirituality and/or religion.

This chapter has addressed in a limited fashion some of the most avoided areas of ministry in the church—those of emotional health and illness. We need to bring this area of life into the church without all the avoidance, superstition, and prejudice of the past. We need to be able to give the church a health checkup and address problematic areas and members in a positive, constructive way. The church has a responsibility, as well as an opportunity, to have a profound affect on those members who manifest unhealthy ways of thinking and being. Thus the church could avoid many of its own crises.

QUESTIONS FOR DISCUSSION/REFLECTION

1. Are religion and spirituality psychological crutches?
2. Do you think a stigma exists in the church regarding mental and emotional illnesses?
3. Is emotional illness ever a sign of lack of faith?
4. What could the church do to minister to those suffering from emotional distress and illness?
5. What are some of the common distorted or incorrect ways of thinking in communities of faith that lead to emotional illness?
6. How does legalism impact mental health?
7. How does absolute freedom from all restraints impact mental health?
8. How does the gospel contribute to good emotional and mental health?
9. What are the characteristics of good spiritual and mental health?
10. How is guilt used destructively in some churches?

Chapter 10

When Churches Walk the Talk

Our society is more fragmented and less connected than in past eras, and one of the most obvious themes in this book is that the church is also beset by its own fragmentation of relationships. The more we can accept this reality, the better we can begin to address and deal with many disappointments in the church. All this should not cause us to be complacent and apathetic about the potential that exists in the church to enhance a person's relationship with God and promote healthy relationships among its members. I maintain that great possibilities exist for churches that are intentional about compassion and want to fill the void in our sense of community and the need for our souls to be relational and have affirming interactions with each other.

In this chapter I briefly consider how the gospel message of the church is still relevant to us and how when the church walks the messages it talks, the potential of the church can be largely realized. I also outline the idea that a healthily functioning church is one that can live faithfully with its humanity. This theoretical model of the church places high priority on the relational dimension of church life.

The concept in the New Testament we call the *gospel* means "good news." This good news means many things, such as God loves us and intervened in our lives in Jesus Christ and continues to intervene in our lives. At its most basic level, the gospel tells us that we are of great worth and that there is a God who has unconditional and unlimited compassion (love) for us and all that we face in this life. This historical message and focusing on the way of Christ is the basis for may important dynamic motivations, answers, and understandings for the Christian and the church.

Although many cultural aspects of the church change and adapt, the foundational relationship characteristics that are manifested in the church, when healthy, appear to me to be much more timeless than various fads to which the church is susceptible today. In fact, it may be fair to state that many disappointments with the church result from some of the "latest and greatest" techniques for programming and growing the church. While we always want to be open to ways of truly enhancing the church, the relational aspects of the gospel cannot be ignored. They cannot be substituted by just any new development, or we may be, as the apostle Paul says in Galatians 1:6, "turning to a different gospel."

The gospel provides an identity by answering the question, "Who am I?" It gives us ethical direction by answering, "How shall I live?" It provides a relationship by answering, "How am I accepted?" It provides a community (the church) by answering "Where do I belong?" A church that is functioning in a healthy manner provides a safe relational environment and context in which the answers to such questions can be found, but more importantly where they can be experienced! When churches walk the talk, they will not talk theology and ignore the practical implications of theology in relationships; instead, their relationships will be congruent with the theology preached and taught. In other words, their behavior in relating will model their theology, not perfectly of course, but experientially one will find the gospel lived out in the community of the church.

Although it will necessitate some repetition, I will now summarize how a healthy church provides vital answers to the questions under consideration. My basic belief is that a church that walks the talk will be intentionally relational in all that it does. By this I mean that relationships will be central to the life of such a church, and in the healthy church one will find many examples of positive, caring, challenging, and loving relationships. The emphasis of the church that is functioning well is not on some ethereal or other-worldly concept, but on the practical integration of the gospel into our ways of relating to God and each other.

THE GOSPEL, AS LIVED IN THE HEALTHY CHURCH, ANSWERS MANY IMPORTANT QUESTIONS

"Who Am I?": Provides Identity

I once saw an old dilapidated bus that had been converted into a camper. Where the destination sign had always been shown in more glorious days of the bus was the word "Nowhere." Sometimes that is the story of our lives, and it has invaded our churches. We question if we are really going anywhere. Many today are wandering aimlessly down the dark hallways that once seemed to be so bright and clear. The society of which they are a part has become complicated and impersonal so that they are without direction.

Our culture has a profound impact on the personal identities of most in our society. The rapidity with which change is progressing leaves few tried and true ways of doing. Many career positions are outdated almost as fast as people complete training for them. Relationships and marriages break up, and familial history and continuity are lost. We are increasingly mobile and relocate frequently.

The church at its best assists us with understanding our identity: We are children of a loving God. This provides a sense of purpose and meaning, of connection with something larger than ourselves, and of worth and destiny. The church should provide us with fertile ground out of which our identities can grow. The gospel states that we are accepted despite our faults; knowing we are accepted and valued is the basis for continued growth and development in life. The apostle Paul put it well in Ephesians 2:19 as translated in the RSV: "So then you are no longer strangers and sojourners, but you are fellow citizens with the saints and members of the household of God."

The church often suffers from identity confusion as well. However, when the church is clear that it is to be a womb for the nurturance and growth of the acceptance of the gospel and when it is intentional about affirming the value of each person, healthy personal and corporate identities are cultivated. Individual churches need to declare their missions and live them. Mission statements, although not the ultimate answer unless implemented and kept as guiding orientations and points of reference, have provided an identity and direction for many churches that are functioning well. In a sea of churches in their community, many churches have carved out their own niche and identity because they have found their own unique mission and focus within the context of the broader gospel message. Some churches minister to the homeless, some accept diversity that is not found in other churches, and others minister to children or the aged. Functional churches have a direction, and they have at least a general plan in place. Healthy churches are always maturing in the realization of their mission and focus, but have the foundational strength of a relational theology of grace. A mission statement without "the mission" of the gospel in place leads to great disappointment with the church.

Those churches that have found their identity as a womb for the growth of relationships that are affirming and accepting provide the environment for people to explore their true selves. They no longer have to hide behind a façade that covers their weaknesses. They no longer have to deny their struggles. The members and visitors can begin to admit to each other their human struggles and failings. The emotional and relational difficulties of human life are not ignored, but are addressed with authenticity and openness. Thereby such characteristics of the human condition can be addressed in a healthy manner, and people can find strength to take corrective actions and to make changes.

None will become perfect, and the problems of human relations will be present, even in healthy churches. However, a process of spiritual, social, psychological, and emotional rebirth and growth occurs. The church when at its best is not just addressing the spiritual striving and failing of people, but the psychological, emotional, and social aspects of identity as well. The church at its best assists us in finding how to better live in all of these areas. In a healthy church these areas are not isolated or divorced from one another, but are all part of an integrated whole. People will be at various levels of maturity and personal development, but all will find themselves in a safe place to be challenged and to grow. Social scientists tell us that identities are, in part, the result of the internalization of the models we witness in our social world. Healthy churches provide the climate for the internalization of healthy relationships, and thus of healthy identities. We discover who we truly are in such a relationally warm and nurturing climate.

"How Shall I Live?": Gives Ethical Direction

One deficit for many people in our current society is that they do not have positive stories or a story from which their life takes direction. In our multimedia age we often no longer listen to oral traditions from our families, communities, and churches. This appears to me to lead to fragmentation and lack of commitment. We do not have a foundation from which to define our lives. Some have only the influence of television or the inner city gang to define who they are. We are lacking in living theology and story as we found in people such as Mother Teresa. Therefore, our behavioral ethics and principles suffer from lack of nourishment and vitality.

The church, as part of its health, provides wonderful stories that have life and vitality. These stories provide direction for our lives. An example of this for the people of Israel is the story about being lead out of Egypt, the Exodus story. The people of Israel were slaves in Egypt when God through Moses brought liberation. This story was often repeated and was a call for Israel to respond to the greatness of God; it gave them an identity as being valued because of God's participation in their lives. There are numerous such stories in the scriptures, and the ultimate story unfolds for the Christian in the New Testament with the story of Jesus Christ. Jesus himself was a storyteller, especially in his parables. Even in the writings of the apostle Paul, we see that his ethics are based or founded on story. In several of the Pauline epistles the authors first sketch out the theology or the story of Christ, and then call us to ethical behavior based on the story of Christ.

There are examples of Jesus taking a much more inclusive approach to how one should live than did the people of his day. His was no legalistic approach. Examples are helping people on the Sabbath and eating grain on the Sabbath. Jesus upset hierarchy. He opposed the status quo. He "spoke as one having authority," yet his power was completely different from the hierarchical authority of his day. He rebelled against limited interpretations and understandings.

Those who formulate a legalist law-based approach to behavior do so by detaching the gospel from Christianity. Our Western culture easily becomes myopic with an overemphasis on law or cheap grace as a means of making things simple; however, this is done as a perversion of the gospel. I believe there are standards, but these must always flow from love and faith.

Churches should always keep the importance of relationship central, and it is my contention that relationship can be a basis for ethical behavior. For the Christian, behavior is not some legalist or monotonous following of a code of conduct, but living in relationship and as a response to the person, Christ. An outgrowth of living in relationship with Christ is learning to live in healthy relationships with each other. This involves the greatest ethical challenge. The church when functioning well will have a balanced approach that promotes and upholds the highest compassionate ethical relationships. In the healthy church relationships will take primacy over technical and legalist approaches that put programs, numerical growth, or financial gain before caring for people. The church is not some cold machine that needs only to be oiled and maintained or revved up by increasing its numbers or financial power; instead, it is a living, vital, relational entity that has a heart and soul.

I have known those who have been extremely orthodox according to their church's view and kept the outward standards of the church, but who did not know the "story" in their hearts and, therefore, were some of the most cold, intolerant, and heartless people I have ever known. We must be compassionate toward such people, but realize they do not represent the message of the church. I believe such persons often have a negative life story that becomes the lens through which they use their religion. The lens distorts and blurs the beauty of the gospel and perverts Christian ethics.

We can be very orthodox, very governed by rules and technical theology and yet miss the essence of being guided by the story of the Christ event. Then we attempt to answer questions no one is asking and miss the hurts and real questions of those around us. This to me is the worst distortion of the Christian life.

The Christian story calls for a broader base for living. The Christian story is not consumed with such perfection, but instead is motivated by the story of love and forgiveness. The story of the Good Samaritan taught by Christ illustrates this well:

> A man was going down from Jerusalem to Jericho, when he fell into the hands of robbers. They stripped him of his clothes, beat him and went away, leaving him half dead. A priest happened to be going down the same road, and when he saw the man, he passed by on the other side. So, too, a Levite, when he came to the place and saw him, passed by on the other side. But a Samaritan, as he traveled, came where

the man was and when he saw him, he took pity on him. He went to him and bandaged his wounds, pouring on oil and wine. Then he put him on his own donkey, took him to an inn and took care of him. The next day he took out two silver coins and gave them to the innkeeper. "Look after him," he said, "and when I return I will reimburse you for any extra expense you may have." Which of these three do you think was a neighbor to the man who fell into the hands of robbers? The expert in the law replied, "The one who had mercy on him." Jesus told him, "Go and do likewise." (Luke 10:30-37)

We must remember that this powerful story was told to people who considered the priest and the Levite to be among the righteous and the Samaritans to be the outcasts. Note that the technical theological experts of the time do not show mercy. The legal expert who at the end answered the question of Christ could not even bring himself to use the word *Samaritan* in his answer. Here we have an interesting paradox of those who were the formal ethicists, those who spent their lives deciding what was or was not proper behavior, being the most unethical of all!

Therefore, we cannot propose that more laws, rules, orthodoxy, technical expertise, or moral theories are what is most needed. These all have their place as guidelines, but they cannot change and motivate the heart. They can be cold and lifeless. Stories, on the other hand, touch our intellect as well as our emotions. Stories approach us in a much more integrated fashion. For Christians, the Christ event or story calls us to live ethically in response to what Christ has done. Then the church at its best can create new stories in its caring and service. The Christian life is not a response to a code of rules or laws or a technical process of church management and life, but a response to Christ and a relationship with Him. This calls for a radical ethic and a radical service to humanity. Churches that walk the talk are seeking and learning to live in this manner.

"How Am I Accepted?": Provides Relationship

Much of what I have already written applies also to this section. I occasionally tell clients in therapy, "What we all desire most of all is love and acceptance, and what we fear most is rejection." The church that is truly talking the talk of the gospel will be proclaiming acceptance; and, of course, it will be walking the walk of accepting all people by its actions.

We might think of how it would feel if most of our friends received a special invitation but we did not. Consider how a little child might feel when not invited to a birthday party, nose pressed against a windowpane, looking and longing, dying to go in, but no one opens the door. Also, we might remember a personal experience such as going on a job search only to be turned down time after time; no one appears to want us, and no one is interested in us. Others may have been rejected by a lover (or can imagine how it would be), consumed with what might have been, feeling that no one in the world can replace the lover in their life. Feelings of rejection, emptiness, and being forsaken come to all of us at times.

Deep in our hearts all of us crave invitation, love, and acceptance and fear exclusion, rejection, and abandonment. The craving for acceptance can vary in intensity because of various life events and life histories; each of us is more or less sensitive to such issues. However, unless we have certain forms of psychological disturbance, the desire to relate is present.

The good news is that God accepts us just as we are and loves us in spite of ourselves. This in turn motivates us toward the good and high road. The gospel tells us that God is interested in a personal relationship with us and invites us to experience this relationship.

The gospel story can reveal to us God's desire for and pursuit of relationship and can be a model for relationships of human origin. Churches should be an oasis of acceptance and love in a world that for many is barren of real relationships. Churches that are healthy are not based on an exclusive theology that sets up barriers to people coming to God. Although there is a natural tendency to be comfortable with others who are similar to us, the church at its best pushes beyond the boundaries of incorporating and ministering to only those who fit the mold of the members. Unfortunately, many churches have established barriers to acceptance and criteria for inclusion. The grace that is found in the New Testament appears to have become a conditional grace for some, which then may become no grace at all. The basis for acceptance in the New Testament is that we accept one another "as Christ accepted us." This leaves no room for superficial exclusion.

If a church is modeling acceptance, it must consider the importance of diversity and how God has shown us great diversity in our world. It is by appreciating the differences among others and learning from them that the church is enhanced. Even though having differences of opinion and belief can be threatening, when modeled in a relational church differences can be energizing. New information is continually coming in, and new ways of looking at old material are developed; thus the church that is healthy lives on the creative edge of processing various ways of understanding. New wine is continually stretching the old wineskins, sometimes exploding them.

Hopefully, many churches are getting back to the foundation of accepting each other and all people based on God's example of acceptance. We do not have to agree with each other to accept each other. Seeing diversity as a spiritual asset not only enhances acceptance in the community, but also allows for the modeling of dealing with disagreements and differences without being disagreeable. This in turn increases the experience of acceptance all the more.

"Where Do I Belong?": Provides Community

Not only do we desire to be in relationship, but we also desire to belong and to be in community. As discussed in Chapter 2, we should not become codependent and find all our identity in an organization. Being a part of a community, however, can be an important adjunct to who we are.

There is great interest in spirituality today, and usual definitions of spirituality include the importance of being in relationship with others and with a higher power or God. In this way our culture states that we are born with a need for connection. Our faith traditions have emphasized the same, although at times only theoretically. The Judeo-Christian religion is not a "lone ranger" type of life. Instead, it is a community-lived experience. Today in the United States we have veered toward a much more individualistic and isolated religious and personal experience, which has carried over into our relationships and families. We too often relate on a superficial level that leaves us feeling empty and shallow. We form relationships to meet our sexual needs or our business or political desires rather than to truly connect with others.

The resulting deficits in our lives leave us more susceptible to feelings of inadequacy, low self-esteem, loneliness, and meaninglessness. A spiritual crisis is created where we do not know who we are or where we belong. We sense a deep longing to be in touch with someone at a more profound level, yet this often eludes us and keeps us grasping for something more.

Churches that talk the talk and walk the walk provide a sense of belonging and community. They state verbally and by their behavior: "You are welcome here. You can find a place to belong here." As emphasized earlier, they do not exclude because a person is not just like them. The inclusive church welcomes one another in diversity because of the common heritage of being created in "the image of God."

Even though one could make a case for disappointment regarding the widespread lack of interest in theology today, a positive result is that the bickering that was so prevalent in the past between denominations is subsiding to a large degree. Not only have churches put up barriers to non-Christians in the past, they have also instituted rigid divisions with other Christians. Churches that are now walking the talk are strong on the unity of fellowship while recognizing the value and richness of diversity. Therefore, members and visitors experience a sense of belonging and community within their midst.

In the healthy church there will be people at various stages of belonging, and they will be accepted. The church will tolerate the various paths people follow on their journey of faith. Some individuals may be on the periphery of the church, checking it out, attempting to assess if it fits for them or not. The healthy church, it appears to me, will always be welcoming but not coercive, always inviting but not demanding.

There will be times during member's lives when they can be more involved in church activities than at others. Too often churches have not been tolerant of family and life situations and unintentionally have forced people to make a choice between church life and family life. This is unfortunate and unnecessary. We need to respect people's right to manage their lives according to the best of their ability. Belonging does not need to be forfeited because of life situations and circumstances. Many people have been disappointed by the lack of understanding of churches when they were attempting to live faithfully within the various needs and circumstances of their lives and the church was intolerant and condemning.

The church at its best is mature enough not to be threatened by the personal and family needs of its members. While issuing a challenge to be faithful to God and to keep our priorities in order, the healthy church does not have to be central to all of life. God should be central to our lives; the church is not God and therefore must assume its rightful place. The healthy church will not assume it is God in the lives of its members. In a relational church, the church will be inviting and attractive based on its character and positive offer to belong instead of demanding and controlling based on its perceived power and authority.

The church when functioning in a healthy manner answers the question "Where do I belong?" by its messages and actions: "You belong in community, you belong in relationship, you belong here if you so choose; we invite you to belong in whatever way you can. We want to assist you on your journey of faith, and we will accept you wherever you are on the journey. We do not expect perfection; we are not perfect as a church. However, we can grow together toward more maturity."

CONCLUSION

In summary, when the church really is the church and when it is walking the walk and talking the talk, it will focus on presenting the gospel story in the language of the day to answer the age-old questions of humankind: "Who am I?" "How shall I live?" "How am I accepted?" "Where do I belong?" These life questions will not be answered in technical and precise terms but will be relevant to the personal and relational needs of the person. Disappointments do not create destructive crises in such contexts. Disappointments concerning human conflicts and differences are greatly lessened when relationships are given primacy in theology, practical teaching, and mentoring. This is the model of a church that faithfully lives to its calling and promotes faithfully living with disappointments in the church. It is a model of the church living with a positive sense of community within our present culture and energized by the vitality that comes from living in authentic relationship with God and each other.

QUESTIONS FOR DISCUSSION/REFLECTION

1. How would you define the gospel to people not in the church?
2. How does the church share the gospel in our current culture? What are central and timeless elements of the gospel?

3. How would you describe "identity"?
4. What does the church tell you about who you are?
5. What does the church tell you about how to live?
6. Should the church be in the business of telling members how to behave and live today?
7. How do you know when someone accepts you?
8. How would you describe "community"?
9. How do we assist people in having a sense of belonging?
10. What are the characteristics of a church that walks the talk?

Epilogue

It is reported that a young person came to Harry Emerson Fosdick and said, "Reverend Fosdick, I no longer believe in God." Fosdick replied, "Tell me about your God. Maybe I don't believe in him either!" In other words, the way some believe about God, their concept of God would leave many *not* believing if their view were the only choice. It is the same with the church. The way some *no longer believe* in the church because of the way they view the church would leave many of us saying, "I don't believe in that either!"

The way many believe in elevating the church is not possible for some of us as well. The extreme concepts of an above-the-clouds, theologically syrupy church and an absolutely nonrelevant church are not the views many of us can ethically accept. A totally divine church would leave us no chance of joining. A totally human church would leave us with little hope of the intervention of God.

Some who are disillusioned with the church are not able to overcome their own resistance to any attachment to an imperfect institution. These hurting people may have an especially difficult time overcoming the disappointment they have experienced. We need to reach out and hear their pain and accept their frustration. They are gun shy and afraid of being hurt again. If you fall into this group, I hope you will give the church a second look; maybe you can take the risk to do so from the standpoint of more realistic expectations than when you made the first approach. The church needs people like you!

Hopefully, all of us can come to a more complete understanding of the church that will lessen some of our disappointment with it. Although it is beset with a multitude of challenges, I continue to believe that it has tremendous potential to awaken once again. The Spirit of God is at work in the church to bring rebirth and resurrection. God has chosen the church to continue the work of Christ in the world, weak, frail, and handicapped by its humanity as it is. Let us not underestimate that which God has chosen. May we be expectant with hope.

Bibliography

Achtemeier, P. (1987). *The Quest for Unity in the New Testament Church.* Philadelphia: Fortress Press.

Brown, R. (1956). *The Significance of the Church.* Philadelphia: Westminster Press.

Campolo, T. (1988). Introduction. In John Fischer (author), *Real Christians Don't Dance* (pp. 7, 8). Minneapolis: Bethany House.

Carus, W. (ed.). (1847). *Memoirs of the Life of Rev. Charles Simeon.* London: J. Hatchard & Son.

Framo, J. (1981). The Integration of Marital Therapy with Sessions with Family of Origin. In Alan Gurman and David Kniskern (eds.), *Handbook of Family Therapy* (pp. 133-158). New York: Bruner/Mazel.

Friedman, E. (1985). *Generation to Generation.* New York: The Guilford Press.

Griffith, J. and Griffith, M. (1992). Therapeutic Change in Religious Families: Working with the God-Construct. In Laurel Burton (ed.), *Religion and the Family* (pp. 63-86). Binghamton, NY: The Haworth Press, Inc.

Hoffer, E. (1951). *The True Believer.* New York: Harper & Row.

Langer, E. (1989). *Mindfulness.* Reading, MA: Addison-Wesley Publishing Company.

Larson, B. (1971). *No Longer Strangers.* Waco, TX: Word Books.

Mason, N. (1982). Editorial. *Good News Unlimited.* Auburn, CA: Good News Unlimited, January, p. 2.

McBride, J. (1989). The Personal Crisis of Denominational Identity. *The Pastoral Forum,* 8(1), pp. 2-3.

McBride, J. (1990). Mistaking Religion for Spirituality. *The Pastoral Forum,* 9(1), pp. 10-11.

McBride, J. (1991). Preventing Burnout Through Spirituality. *The Counselor,* 9(3), pp. 10-13.

McBride, J. (1998). *Spiritual Crisis: Surviving Trauma to the Soul.* Binghamton, NY: The Haworth Press, Inc.

McBride, J. (1999). When the Community Stumbles. *The Pastoral Forum,* 17, (1/2) pp. 11-12.

Miller, K. (1965). *The Taste of New Wine.* Waco, TX: Word Books.

Moltmann, J. (1978). *The Open Church: Invitation to a Messianic Lifestyle.* London: SCM Press.

Narramore, S. (1984). *No Condemnation.* Grand Rapids, MI: Zondervan Publishing House.

Nelson, W. (1974). *Liberation.* Chicago: Covenant Publications.

Oates, W. (1978). *The Religious Care of the Psychiatric Patient.* Philadelphia: Westminster Press.

Oates, W. (1987). *Behind the Masks.* Philadelphia: Westminster Press.

Outler, A. (ed.) (1985). Catholic Spirit. Sermons 34-70, 1771. *The Works of John Wesley,* Vol. 2 (pp. 81-91). Nashville, TN: Abingdon Press.

Perry, L. and Shawchuck, N. (1982). *Revitalizing the 20th Century Church.* Chicago: Moody Bible Institute.

Schaef, A. (1988). *When Society Becomes an Addict.* San Francisco: Harper & Row.

Schaef, A. and Fassel, D (1988). *The Addictive Organization.* San Francisco: Harper & Row.

Seligman, M. (1990). *Learned Optimism.* New York: Simon & Schuster (Pocket Book Edition).

Snodgrass, K. (1990). *Between Two Truths: Living with Biblical Tensions.* Grand Rapids, MI: Zondervan Publishing House.

Tillich, P. (1952). *The Courage to Be.* New York: Vail-Ballou Press, Inc.

van Rooyen, S. (1983). Is the Church a Hole in the Head? *Unraveling Some Ideas.* Auburn, CA: Good News Unlimited, pp. 17-24.

Wesley, N. (1974). *Liberation.* Chicago: Covenant Publications.

Wilke, R. (1986). *And Are We Yet Alive? The Future of the United Methodist Church.* Nashville, TN: Abingdon Press.

Xavier, N. (1987). *The Two Faces of Religion.* Tuscaloosa, AL: Portals Press.

Index

Page numbers followed by the letter "e" indicate exhibits.

Order a copy of this book with this form or online at:
http://www.haworthpress.com/store/product.asp?sku=5355

LIVING FAITHFULLY WITH DISAPPOINTMENT IN THE CHURCH

_____in hardbound at $39.95 (ISBN-13: 978-0-7890-2621-7; ISBN-10: 0-7890-2621-X)

_____in softbound at $14.95 (ISBN-13: 978-0-7890-2622-4; ISBN-10: 0-7890-2622-8)

Or order online and use special offer code HEC25 in the shopping cart.

COST OF BOOKS_____

POSTAGE & HANDLING_____
(US: $4.00 for first book & $1.50
for each additional book)
(Outside US: $5.00 for first book
& $2.00 for each additional book)

SUBTOTAL_____

IN CANADA: ADD 7% GST_____

STATE TAX_____
(NJ, NY, OH, MN, CA, IL, IN, PA, & SD
residents, add appropriate local sales tax)

FINAL TOTAL_____
(If paying in Canadian funds,
convert using the current
exchange rate, UNESCO
coupons welcome)

☐ **BILL ME LATER:** (Bill-me option is good on
US/Canada/Mexico orders only; not good to
jobbers, wholesalers, or subscription agencies.)

☐ Check here if billing address is different from
shipping address and attach purchase order and
billing address information.

Signature_____

☐ **PAYMENT ENCLOSED: $**_____

☐ **PLEASE CHARGE TO MY CREDIT CARD.**

☐ Visa ☐ MasterCard ☐ Amex ☐ Discover
☐ Diner's Club ☐ Eurocard ☐ JCB

Account #_____

Exp. Date_____

Signature_____

Prices in US dollars and subject to change without notice.

NAME_____

INSTITUTION_____

ADDRESS_____

CITY_____

STATE/ZIP_____

COUNTRY_____ COUNTY (NY residents only)_____

TEL_____ FAX_____

E-MAIL_____

May we use your e-mail address for confirmations and other types of information? ☐ Yes ☐ No
We appreciate receiving your e-mail address and fax number. Haworth would like to e-mail or fax special
discount offers to you, as a preferred customer. **We will never share, rent, or exchange your e-mail address
or fax number.** We regard such actions as an invasion of your privacy.

Order From Your Local Bookstore or Directly From
The Haworth Press, Inc.
10 Alice Street, Binghamton, New York 13904-1580 • USA
TELEPHONE: 1-800-HAWORTH (1-800-429-6784) / Outside US/Canada: (607) 722-5857
FAX: 1-800-895-0582 / Outside US/Canada: (607) 771-0012
E-mail to: orders@haworthpress.com

For orders outside US and Canada, you may wish to order through your local
sales representative, distributor, or bookseller.
For information, see http://haworthpress.com/distributors

(Discounts are available for individual orders in US and Canada only, not booksellers/distributors.)

PLEASE PHOTOCOPY THIS FORM FOR YOUR PERSONAL USE.
http://www.HaworthPress.com   BOF04